An Insignificant Boy

A memoir

by Chris Middleton

The Conrad Press

An Insignificant Boy

Published by The Conrad Press in the United Kingdom 2023

Tel: +44(0)1227 472 874
www.theconradpress.com
info@theconradpress.com

ISBN 978-1-916966-14-7

Typesetting and Cover Design by: Levellers, Cover design and illustrations Chris Middleton

The Conrad Press logo was designed by Maria Priestley.

Printed and bound in Great Britain by Clays Ltd, Elcograf S.p.A.

The final broadcast of Radio Clix. A memoir of a space-age childhood through the eyes of an unusual boy with ageing, war-damaged parents. What they did to him. And how his imagination helped him survive.

Contents

There are some griefs so loud
They could bring down the sky
And there are griefs so still
None knows how deep they lie.

– May Sarton

Everything you love is very likely to be lost.
But in the end, love will return in a different way.

– Franz Kafka

All my life I have felt like a foreign correspondent, a
stranger in a strange land reporting back on the things he
sees. Only when I travel does this feeling occasionally
make sense and I experience a brief sense of belonging
from being an alien and outsider. But my disconnection
remains when I return home. The truth is, I have never
belonged anywhere, except in the world of music and
books.
This memoir explains why.

– Chris Middleton

'Yes, we do have nightmares. But we also have dreams.'

– Frank Capra

Foreword

Hello. My name is Christopher.

As a little boy, my parents nicknamed me 'Clicky'[1] – 'Clix' for short. I was always tapping out rhythms and, as a baby, clicking the brightly coloured plastic keys that hung above my pram.

You will meet that boy in a moment, because he is putting on a play for you, as he always loved to do. It is a tragedy, and a comedy of the darkest hue. But in the end, also a tale of hope, redemption, and love.

Clix so loved to tell stories – with toy theatres and puppets, with masks and makeup, spinning and jumping in front of the class.

There: can you see him?

Bookends

SUNFLOWER

Once, when my friend Danny and I were eighteen, we got hopelessly drunk and decided to drive his car as fast as we could down rural lanes in the engine-black night. We lived in the hinterland between town and country, between memory and forgetting.

So, we set off, laughing at our luck at being alive in this moment, taking it in turns to swig from a half bottle of scotch as he floored the accelerator. Oh, it was thrilling to be at the side of a dangerous friend. School was out and we were free forever, two grown-ups driving towards amnesia.

As we hit a bend at ninety-five, Danny lost control of the car and it tipped up on two wheels, struck an embankment and spun through a hedge, finally coming to rest on its side in a field beneath the moon. Incredibly, we were unhurt and, being Danny's car, of course there was not a scratch on it. Proof that we were indestructible.

Years later, motor neurone disease would make him close up like a sunflower at dusk, until my bright, golden friend vanished forever. But on that night in our grass-scented youth, we laughed and cheered at the crash, clambered out through the window, pushed the car back onto its wheels in the hot, dry earth, and drove off.

But by the time we pulled up near my parents' house, the shock of what had happened hit me and I had a panic attack. I began to keen and shake in the passenger seat, staring ahead at the moth-flecked streetlights and the mist of September's coming. "D-D-Dan," I said. *"Help me."*

Danny nodded to himself, switched off the engine, then turned to me and smiled – patiently, as he often did, like he was dealing with a simpleton. "Chris… Chris… *Chris*," he whispered. *"Live a little.* We're only young once."

The stories that follow are the things my friend never knew, but perhaps sometimes guessed.

Act One

The Man Who Shouted at the Sky

If time ran backwards, our words would speak us.

Picture a pretty boy with brown hair and blue eyes, a child who is always laughing.

Clix is perhaps twelve at this moment and rides a noisy wooden skateboard, down past the mound of a ruined castle. Now he nods in his room, reading *Dandelion Wine* by Ray Bradbury as an old reel-to-reel tape recorder[2] un-spools. Now he makes a longbow from bamboo and slings it on his back, running into the beech trees. Now he rides a bike in circles around Owen, the friend he has snatched it from, who looks at him, half smiling. They fight on the grass – Owen wins – then lie next to each other, pointing up at the screaming swifts.

At dusk, the boy trudges back to a door at the end of a long, dark path garlanded with flowers, his head down and shoulders drooping. The door flies open and a bespectacled figure scowls at him from the shadows, tuts, then walks back to his study. That angry man is my father. I have come home.

When he died in 2021, my sister and I tried to find Dad in old photographs, like archaeologists piecing together some remnant of a lost civilisation. He was certainly that. Our father was a standing stone, now fallen; once part of a circle, now buried alone on an Oxfordshire hillside. I believe it was what he wanted all along; to be solitary.

He spent his declining years writing about the Rollright Stones and mapping the paths of sun and moon. Joanna said that, just before he passed, he saw visions of a golden web floating above his head, as if the universe had come to claim him.

Many years before I was born, pictures of Dad from the 1950s reveal a dapper young architect, a clothes horse, almost a dandy. A man who projected warmth, intelligence, sincerity – even a hint of adventure. I can see why Mum fell for that version of him; the romantic letters he sent her, written in italic script on parchment, seemed so charming and confident. A gentleman, it seemed.

Some in our family encountered that person over the years and have fond memories of him from Christmases past – moments that are precious to me too for their rarity and beauty. But others met a very different man to the aesthete in those photographs. I am one of them.

One day some cousins visited: warm, funny relatives of my mother, who I always loved to see. Dad was charm itself and welcoming, but as soon as they left, he hissed, "You have no idea what *torture* it is for me to meet *people like that*," then stormed back to his charts and manuscripts. That was when I learned how easy it was for him to deceive our rare visitors, to hypnotise them with politeness. And so, our beautiful afternoon was undone.

– But few people ever came.

By the time my childhood world was captured in 1970s colour, Mum and Dad's relationship had faded to black and white. Every day they sat in separate rooms with their backs to the door, only meeting in the hallway to scream at each other. Their relationship was like a Weald storm, trapped and circling in the valley between North and South Downs. Out in the garden, Mum fought to hold the clapping white sheets on the line.

This was the father I knew: solitary, remote, friendless, and silent – Saturnine and above reproach, yet full of it himself. An autodidact committed to astronomy, science, history, and art; private passions that I shared. But also, one who was tormented and in mysterious mental pain, raging like King Lear on the blasted heath. A man who once climbed a ladder to shout at the sky.

And then there was Mum, obstinate and strong, with her eternal love of royalty and the ballet: an unmoveable object living with an irresistible force. One Easter, Dad gave her a vinyl record of romantic songs. She sneered at it, and he crumpled it into a ball with rage.

My parents seemed war-torn and damaged from events long before I was born; cracked and empty, ready to fill with each other's ire and sadness. Perhaps I was brought into the world to fix them, to restore them from whatever explosions had buried them in the rubble and dust of the past...

I failed. But at least I won over my big sister, who was seven years older and so one life-step ahead; just far enough to escape them when I was still at school. Her own childhood in Folkestone had been more idyllic, playing in Kingsnorth Gardens while the Golden Arrow steamed past on the railway bridge, covering Mum's sheets in soot.

I was born there by the sea, in a four-floor house that had once held a dance studio. But before I was three, we moved seventy miles inland. There, we found ourselves becalmed in Reigate, a small, empty town beneath a hill, in another big house. This one was in a walled private garden, overhung by an elm that was full of faces at night.

Our horizons vanished behind the whispering, haunted tree. I grew up in its shadow, secluded, down a long path away from people: *Clicky and the tree of ghosts*. A giant poplar stood behind the house; we were guarded.

It was an infinite regress of seclusion, of first-class train compartments and private boxes at the theatre, of the hush and fold of stern-voiced newspapers. Until I went to school, I'm not sure I had even *seen* another child my age. But with my binoculars in the window, I caught glimpses of the hollow town, as solitude, eyeless, hid the stars in its branches.

– At times I was not a boy, but the headlights of cars on an ill-used road; the mail train's roar at midnight; the gaunt, creaking timbers of fear, of night descending the staircase unwanted. The absence before the thought, then the thought itself. Clix, the idea of a child, sleepless and frightened in his father's arms, carried back to bed in search of dreams. Old voices calling on the edge of airwaves, melodies lost in tenebrous static. Restless and shivering, with Tansy bear at his side, and his Magnavox yo-yo radio.

And so, my parents' long war raged on. Day after day I sat alone in my room, discovering new ways to pass the time, soon an only child by circumstance. I taught myself to draw cartoons, to paint in oils and watercolours; to write sketches, poems, and short stories; to play guitar and keyboards; to compose pop songs and classical pieces; to use a camera, and tinker with ancient gramophones and loudspeakers.

Aged eight, I built a primitive sampler from the cylinder of an old Dictaphone and began experimenting with quadrophonic sound, tape loops, and echo. I designed balsa hovercraft and flew them across the garden. I wrote film scripts, launched imaginary products, and drew illustrated books full of monsters and fantastic creatures. I made a stop-motion King Kong to fight my Johnny Apollo astronaut – frame by captured frame. Soon friends brought broken toys for me to mend, to young Professor Branestawm and his soldering iron.

I was lucky. I found a universe within me, unbidden; an infinite space of dreams and ideas, as Mum and Dad fought and argued in the hall below, forgetting their studious son. It was that or submit to the haunted, troubled house, and I refused to let its sadness in. So, I invented myself from whatever discarded items I could find in the junk shop of a solitary heart.

These were the things I carried forward in life, and so the child created the man who is talking to you now. He invented me, so I might pull him towards the future; or perhaps he gave *me* a future instead. Clix willed himself to live – to be happy while battle raged, or his father looked at maps of the stars and his mother sat desolate in the kitchen.

He planted a pine cone in his parents' garden, and it grew into a tree[3].

Far from the forest of others.

****

So, who was my father? Joanna believes she saw him in a documentary about the wartime codebreakers at Bletchley Park – a glimpse in another old photograph. Was he really part of Alan Turing's team[4]? That may be a deeper question than anyone can answer. Dad was a code that neither my sister nor I ever cracked. He was an enigma, yet never a cypher; with dots of compassion, but dashes of rage.

He would sit alone in his study for days, poring over building designs, journals, and maps of the stars. It was a universe he never shared with anyone, but I admired him for living in it: architect and astronomer to his regal self; sidereal, elysian, and esoteric. In my father's realm, the highest heaven was full of fire and wonder, yet also cold, remote, and empty.

We know he spent two years as a young man, just twenty, with the Occupation Force in post-war Japan. Dad was stationed in Hiroshima in 1946, only months after the bomb had dropped. He crossed half the world in a troop ship to stand in an atomic wasteland.

What horrors did he witness there? He would never say, so we can only guess at how *we* might have felt at the erasure of a city: an explosion so hot and bright it left people's shadows on walls, and others disfigured and burned. The dawn of the Atomic Age – and of our nuclear family.

We talk of the heroism of the war generation, but overlook the damage. In my father's case, lifelong claustrophobia and tinnitus, and, at times, an ashen, petrified silence. He never wanted to travel overseas again; two years in Hiroshima and he had seen enough for a lifetime. Thus, his family became shadows on a wall in suburban England.

At least, that's one explanation. But that's the problem with enigmas; they make you fill the emptiness with your own thoughts and dreams. You project them into the void, in the vain hope of an echo.

From Dad there was only silence; or a hiss of contempt for anyone who interrupted his solitary travails, as if nothing and no one could charm him. Yet he professed a lifelong admiration for the Japanese: for their asceticism, minimalism, and devotion to duty. Mum – war damaged too, and neglected – shared that pursuit of duty, but filled the house with trinkets.

Look at the night sky, as Dad loved to do, and most of what you see is an absence: a missing father. The billions of galaxies, stars, and planets – the observable universe – are less than five percent of the stuff that must be there for that universe to exist.

Dad could have told you that twenty-seven percent of the universe is dark matter, so called because we just can't see it; we only know it is there because light bends around it. He was like that himself: present, yet somehow unobservable; always in the house, but never in the home.

A final calculation gives us a startling fact: sixty-eight percent of the universe is a vacuum filled with dark energy, the force that pushes things apart. Dad had that too, the ability to dismantle people with a smirk, a curse, a turned shoulder. An unknowable man whose silence left you to find fault with yourself.

The problem is, the more you push things apart, the colder the universe becomes. And anyone who looks at the stars is really gazing into the distant past in a slow search for meaning, to find their place in the present. But I understood my father's quest. After all, many middle-class families are rootless, disconnected from any real pasts of their own. I certainly am.

So, perhaps those of us who gather at the solstice[5] represent the five percent of the cosmos that huddles together for warmth, light, companionship, and love. We are lucky because we can do that. But it was not a choice that seemed open to my father, who would twist and contort his face to stop himself from laughing at *Fawlty Towers*.

– Musn't show your feelings.

The messy world of emotions seemed strange, at times even frightening to him: his rising panic when things were not clipped, clear-cut, dutiful, and regimented. A crumbling of paternalism into rage. Yet most of it was directed at himself; that was the enduring mystery. An ascetic locked in battle with the forces of heart and mind.

– So, what were they? What demons possessed my father? I would find out soon enough. But all that is to come, much later in my story.

Blood, siblings, family, togetherness... such ideas meant nothing to him. They were cosmic accidents, he said; mere fripperies of "the lower orders". A troubling phrase I found in his journals – written by a man who left school at fourteen when war broke out over such ideas. But logarithms, the Golden Ratio and the orbits of the spheres? These were where real beauty and mystery lay: divine proportion, a higher order of consciousness, the universe of maths.

Control was everything to Dad, and timetables too. Perhaps that's why he loved trains so much: he had an attic full of them, so I had to climb a ladder to reach him in his heavenly vault of wood, clockwork, and tin, another private space beneath the stars. It always felt like an intrusion: the magus at play, conjuring alchemical spells from tinplate.

One long summer, he published a book on railway stations: places of arrival or departure, but never destinations. As a boy at infant school, I was impressed that my father was now an author, and a photographer to boot. He returned to writing in his declining years, with a booklet on HG Wells' life in Folkestone[6].

Dad was a time machine. He could map the stars and planets, and make orreries – intricate models of the solar system. He would build zoetropes and mechanisms that revealed the tilt of the Earth's axis, all covered in his jagged italic script. But they were always gifts to himself, display pieces of his mastery of planetary mechanics.

It was the same hand that filled notebooks with equations, with thoughts on Einstein's universe. But the quanta of the heart were invisible to him, its emotions spooky, distant, and indecipherable. Dad could draw up a plan for a building, but not, alas, for a home. His was the blueprint of a heart, its outline.

Yet despite his strangeness, there was much I admired about him. His passion for architecture, his vocation. He filled his study with paintings, and with books on relativity, art, ancient magick, history, time, and poetry.

It was a room I crept into when he was at work, to discover Paul Klee, Frank Lloyd Wright, *The Golden Bough*, Jacob Epstein, Eric Gill, Cézanne, TS Eliot, and Le Corbusier for myself. As a boy, I felt like a Kandinsky in a world full of Rothkos – neurons firing, brain fizzing with ideas, stories, poetry, and song. The tree of ghosts at my window.

My father's shelves contained hundreds of theatre programmes and old ballet books too – my mother's from Sadler's Wells and the Royal Opera House – so my schooling leapt from Einstein and Dirac to Nijinsky and *The Rite of Spring*. I came to see it all as the same dance.

Dad took me to the public library, and pointed me towards Sherlock Holmes, and Ted Hughes' *The Iron Man*. Both revealing choices: stories about a dysfunctional logician, and a boy who must piece together a broken machine from another world.

He gave me Ray Bradbury's *The Illustrated Man*, an excellent gift; those fantastic tales lit the flame of literature in me, leading me to Poe, Melville, Joyce, Faulkner, Steinbeck, Flannery O'Connor, and Virginia Woolf. I devoured *The Waves*, *To the Lighthouse*, *Dubliners*, and *Moby Dick*, all 'golden apples of the sun'.

But my father also handed me *Dracula* one night, in the library that I loved; the tale of an ancient vampire trapped in a castle, casting no reflection. I should have paid attention.

Together, we went to old Mr La Trobe's toyshop, a magickal, dark emporium full of puppets and November fireworks. It was hidden down a cobbled alley[7] behind his sister's, Miss La Trobe's, haberdashery and general store. There, I could choose robots, skateboards, Dinky Toys, and Gerry Anderson spaceships, all things I adored in the private realm I was building in my bedroom: Ideal Zeroids, *UFO* Interceptors, a Surf Flier deck. A pop-culture mirror to my father's empty cosmos; an infinity of fun.

At times I felt I was living in Bradbury's universe, my Converse sneakers pounding the summer streets: *Famous Monsters of Filmland*, bubble-gum cards of *This Island Earth*, Ray Harryhausen movies, *How and Why Wonder Books*, *Tomorrow's World*, and Hammer films with Cushing and Lee. I loved them all. But they were just... *things*. In the absence of love, I became a collector.

Television – such as the huge, ancient set I bought at a jumble sale for 50 pence, dragged home on my go-kart, and coaxed back to life in my room – was my portal to a Modernist dream. *Thunderbirds, Captain Scarlet, Stingray*, and *Space 1999*: a world of vermillion rockets and neoteric cities; a realm of infinite invention in the brown and orange cosiness of a 1970s small town. My parents' Edwardian lives seemed dull by comparison with Destiny Angel, monorails, and Joe 90 – 'the boy who could be anyone'; I felt that way too.

Voyage to the Bottom of the Sea, Jacques Cousteau, and *Barrier Reef* left memories of the ocean silted in my blood: the seaside childhood I should have had. But now there was a deeper place in my heart for *Belle and Sebastian*, *White Horses*, and *The Adventures of Robinson Crusoe*: tales of a lonely boy among snow-capped mountains, a stable full of circling stallions, and a man stranded on a desert island. Even their theme music spoke to me – of solace and escape.

Then one night, alone in my room, I saw Kate Bush sing *The Man with the Child in His Eyes*, and fell asleep with my arms around the timeworn, glowing set. That scrying glass full of dusty valves and old magick, it brought the world to me. And beauty.

TV chat shows with eminent men replaced family conversation – unless my parents were fighting, of course. I knew more about Eric Morecambe and Sammy Davis Jr than I did about my father or his mysterious relatives: the grandfather who made cryptic jigsaws; the uncle who understood soundwaves and lived alone in a cottage full of Chinese artefacts and Roman gods; Dad's absent sisters and their families, any mention of whom would make him storm from the room. Those women who had disagreed with him once, and so were cast out forever.

– A man who, in his thirties, once sat up all night with a shattered arm rather than bother my aunt and uncle, from whom he was renting a room. (He had fallen off a ladder and smashed every bone, while they were downstairs talking.) Next morning, he walked to hospital in silent agony. Good husband material for my middle-aged mother, they thought.

With Dad's back always turned, I would surf the channels for role models, searching the static for signals about what kind of man an isolated boy could become: James Bond or Doctor Who, perhaps – a suave assassin or a thief of time. ("The Seen Connery film is on!" shouted my schoolfriend Ian, ejecting baddies from his Corgi DB5. "It's *Sean*," I explained. But Ian's arm was scarred from the saucepan of boiling water his mother would pour on it, so we agreed on 'Seen'.)

Should I be principled, upstanding, and brave, like James Stewart and Sidney Poitier? A polymath and raconteur, like David Niven and Orson Welles? A fighter-philosopher like Ali, or a clown with a calculus heart, like Jerry Lewis? Should I wear a trench coat in the shadows like Michael Caine, or dance my shadow across the desert like Peter O'Toole? I had no idea. And no concept of how *odd* any of this was.

I assembled myself from clues in books, magazines, comics, and films. It never occurred to me to be normal, because I lacked that frame of reference. I lived in an empty town where backs were turned, and a dark house full of ghosts, silence, astrolabes, and star charts, ruled by a wounded narcissist.

Then I met Owen, the boy from almost-next-door, just a tennis ball's throw from our garden. He grounded me – literally, by hurling me in the dust, sitting on me, and laughing at my madness. How could I not love such a friend?

Owen gifted me normality, kinship, adventure, and vandalism; the kind of boyhood I thought only existed in Mark Twain. I watched him in wonder, as he oiled his bike chain, wrestled with handlebars, and leapt off walls. Of course, my mother hated him, this common lad from Earth.

Yet still I was lost in space. My father theorised about the cold, empty cosmos, but I wanted to fill it with warmth, light, and people. And above all, with friends. As Will Robinson's secret brother[8], I loved astronauts, and Buzz Aldrin the most. They were always on TV, jumping slowly in the moondust – in that magnificent desolation where there was nothing, not even air. I understood them, I saw their loneliness; I lived on the moon too.

On the day Apollo 11 landed in the Sea of Tranquillity, there was a loud buzzing noise from our TV when a caption flashed onscreen, as Aldrin danced before the camera. Sitting in my mother's lap, I asked, "What was that?", as our ancient telly grizzled and crackled at the words blazing there before us, a common fault with old black-and-white sets.

"That's just caption buzz," said Mum, imperious in her armchair, "it's nothing to worry about, dear." But I misheard her and for years afterwards believed Captain Buzz was named for his ability to make our television vibrate with pleasure from a distance of two hundred and forty thousand miles.

And so, at the age of five, I fell in love with an astronaut: a man a quarter of a million miles more distant than my father, yet somehow more present in the room. Years later I told this story to a friend. Next morning a handmade card fell onto my doormat, a picture of my hero standing alone in the dust. Inside were just three words: 'Captain Buzz, forever'.[9]

As a boy, I wanted to fly away too, to leave the Earth behind. So, Dad and I went to air shows to watch Victors, Buccaneers, Vulcans, and Lightnings. We climbed hills to fly the kites or balsawood Phantoms he made and escape the gravity between us. He would labour for weeks alone in his study and emerge with a box kite, a Chinese dragon, a flying monoplane – more loving gifts to himself that I could watch him throw into the sky. Yet still I was earthbound.

We played cricket in the garden, just like a real father and son, and rode the Bluebell Line on ancient steam trains into the rolling fields of England. We fished for stickleback and frogspawn, and I wrestled the wooden go-cart he built for me down gentle inclines, on wheels plucked from my sister's pram. Johnny Apollo in his moon buggy.

It was a heroic effort, but Dad was always as silent as an automaton, so I felt desperate and lonely among the thrilling, beautiful machines – sometimes even frightened. What did his silence mean?

And some days he took me to the Castle Grounds and into the trees, then rewarded me with a toy – from La Trobe's at the foot of the ancient Crown Steps. Those moments are a blank. I have few memories of walks with my father; at least, not beyond the trees.

Perhaps that is because he was always a firmly closed book – one slammed shut with a curse if anyone came near – so I never felt a deep connection with him. His universe was cold, silent, and always receding from me, or glimpsed from afar in his wizard's library.

Or perhaps there is another explanation. For years I had day-terrors, dark daydreams about a shadow-man standing above me in the undergrowth; and my collection of toys was growing. Years later, the memory of one of those walks would return. But all that is to come.

For now, I knew one thing: Dad was acting the role of father from some distant, lonely place – among the ghosts of a vapourised city, perhaps. A wordless man, his wisdom and feelings forever shut away in the slow troop ship to Armageddon. Memories that, to any middle-aged person, would have seemed close enough to touch. *Relativity*.

One moonlit night in my early teens, he drove me to a travelling fair, which flashed and glittered beneath loss-enchanted stars. He didn't speak on the journey, of course, and refused to come on the rides. So, I sat alone on the dodgems, the waltzer, and the big wheel, trying to look happy for him as he watched: two solitary strangers in the October country.

Lights spun, music pounded and surged, families laughed and shrieked with pleasure. Then we drove home in silence, beneath a ragged paper moon.

In such moments, I would dream that Captain Buzz was watching from afar, waving at me for reassurance as he stood with his flag and NASA box-brownie. But at that point in life, my hero had problems of his own: Aldrin was a drunk selling used cars in the great American desert.

But Dad knew how to wear a jacket, to *look* the part. My father the architect, his eyes grey musket balls – ancient, blunt, and wounding. See him: striding stiff-legged across the lawn, making divider-like movements. Measuring, always searching. But for what?

The secret to unlock the universe.

****

So, we were marooned as a family. Or rather, our ghostship had run aground in the Surrey hills, with just the memory of water to lift it.

My father's solitary obsessions meant he wasn't just absent from *my* life, much of the time, but also from Mum's, and from Joanna's. He cut himself off from his sisters and their families[10], who I didn't know; from his own father, who I met just once (he said nothing as we walked around town); and from the granddaughter and son-in-law Dad disowned for being black, despite his love of Duke Ellington, Ella Fitzgerald, and Billie Holliday. He blanked my African brother-in-law and niece for four decades, turning his back if they entered the room.

My father was the type of man Holliday sang about; one who might have seen 'strange fruit hanging from the poplar trees' and thought it good, 'blood on the leaves and blood at the root'. ("I wish Africa would sink in the sea," he once said.)

Yet despite these horrors, he could be sensitive and principled – sometimes even brave. Aged fifteen, for example, Dad volunteered to be a firewatcher at St Paul's Cathedral during the Blitz. He put himself in mortal danger to protect the building he loved; I am proud of that.

When told he was too young to go to war – with his poor eyesight and high blood pressure – the trainee boy-architect downed tools in the office and sat at his drawing board all night in silent protest, staring into space. I can imagine it now: wordless, simmering and resentful, his back turned: the very man he later became. *How dare anyone say no to him! To the universal codebreaker and self-crowned king!*

Yet when working for a wealthy but arrogant client in his retirement, Dad asked for a rose as payment for weeks of architectural work. There's beauty in that. But roses? I only see the thorns. You will find out why later.

When I left home in the early 90s after Mum disowned me for being gay – "You are not my son," she said, rolling her eyes like Norma Desmond – Dad put his head around the door as I was packing my bag. He said Mum's words were "nothing that he thought or felt", then muttered something about the Ancient Greeks. I like to think that he was telling me I was his son and he loved me. Shouting into the void again, still hoping for an echo.

Then Dad told me I was "lucky to live in a world where I could just be myself". It wasn't true, of course; Mum had proved it. But could *he* not be himself in some way? This man who was truer to his will than anyone, no matter the cost?

"I see too deeply into the nature of things," he once wrote in his journal, next to his notes about Fibonacci, Einstein, and the Golden Ratio. But love was the one universal concept that my father just couldn't grasp – at least, not openly – while my mother tried to and failed. But their children could. And we did, though that would be years in the future for both of us.

But one thing was clear, to me and everyone who knew me. As Danny put it one day in the 1980s as we strode down that long, dark path garlanded with flowers to my parents' front door: "Chris, *you do know* you live in a madhouse?"

I laughed, but I remember thinking: a savant living with a disappointed woman? A racist father with a black son-in-law, and a homophobic, ballet-obsessed mother raising a secretly gay son, keeping up appearances for no one in an empty town? Of course, I could see the absurdity: it was a tale of complete middle-class dysfunction.

But I just said, "*Yes*, Dan. *I know*."

Then Dad opened the door to me and my blonde, sporty, handsome young schoolfriend, who beamed at him like a wonky Kevin Costner. And something very strange happened.

My father smiled.

Bookends

CHRISTMAS

The December before he died, Dad built a huge Advent calendar for himself out of card and wood, a tableau depicting a man walking alone across a snow-covered winter landscape.

Each day he would move the figure one step further along, leaving a trail of tiny footsteps behind it in the model snow. When it finally reached Christmas, he simply pushed it off the edge.

– Dad knew his own days were numbered; that he was falling off the world.

At Christmas in my childhood, he gave me robots that walked tall and proud. Their faces lit up more than his did, though their hearts were just tin and cogwheels. He gave machines that sparked in the dark, powerful torches, fluorescent toys… so many sources of light.

One year it was a treasure chest of candescence, and an American steam locomotive that hooted and chuffed with lamps ablaze. Perhaps he was illuminating my way towards escape, towards a brighter life somewhere. *Casey Jones and Junior on the Cannonball Express.*

How strange, then, that only darkness, silence, and rage came from him in person. Except at Christmas, when he mellowed in the horsehair armchair and smiled at my aunt in her ranch-style Sixties home: all mod cons, radiogram, and plush walnut cabinets. An acre of land; a forest.

She would shout *"Christopher!"* from the kitchen, my uncle would be funny and bluff, and my cousin would roar up in the MG he had brought back from rust: soft tires on gravel as the old clock tocked and chimed.

I'd lie under Yuletide stars and imagine a laughing man made of frost and inner warmth, leading the Wild Hunt across the sky: the Spirit of Winter. One Christmas night I'm sure I heard him in the sleeping house, where bedclothes smelled of linen, distant pipe-smoke, and a Labrador's forehead. And we'd hear stories of my grand uncle, the composer Herbert Howells, and his actress daughter Ursula.

"Haslemere three six five six?" My aunt's voice on the telephone to her friends and neighbours.

Before then, as Advent began, I would dig up the noble fir from *our* garden, and garland it with tinsel, crescent moons, scuffed silver birds, and frosted baubles. I'd squint to make the tree-lights sparkle, then ring a mercury-glass bell to summon the Spirit. Three tin angels span on the mantel.

At school, Greg Lake's voice would soar above boys' shouts in the snowy halls, and sing, *"I wish you a hopeful Christmas, I wish you a brave new year. All anguish, pain, and sadness, leave your heart and let your road be clear."* And I would smile to myself and thank him.

On Christmas Eve we would drive to my aunt's house in the countryside, nestled like a fox in the dark-wintered woods. And I would know that, for three whole days, we would do something truly magickal: sit together in the same room. Like a family.

Bookends

MR LEE FORGETS

From their lightships and stormy platforms, pirate DJs broadcast exciting songs into my pre-school years, on airwaves that had long seemed windblown, night-woven, and saccharine. The World Service, Hilversum, and the Light Programme, soon they were swept aside by the psychedelic noise of Radio Caroline, of singles like *Paper Sun, My White Bicycle,* and *See Emily Play*. It was glorious.

Television showed me the world in monochrome, but it was music that filled it with colour. Pop songs taught me that love was blue, and that moons were pink; that Tuesdays were ruby and submarines yellow; that kites were snow-white and lettered with gold, scattered like rice-paper stars in my heaven. Then came Bowie, Kraftwerk, disco, and punk: a world of outrage, strangeness, charm, and glamour; of Sparks and Kate Bush; of gratuitous sax and senseless violins.

The music room at middle school had a staid, gold ceiling, but Grieg's *In the Hall of the Mountain King* conjured a darkness and wild abandon that I loved. Mr Lee – gentle and summoned, like a chubby Hugh Grant in a corduroy jacket – smiled and notched up the volume in our sunlit haven, hidden from the sunken garden and the silent stone gryphons that guarded the playground. My teacher was quiet and hidden too, but dressed eloquently in thought.

And, like me, Mr Lee was animated by the dramatic sound of a powerful hi-fi.

As a boy, I sat arranged at pianos, my ivory fingers thumping the keys. But as soon as I held a guitar for the first time, something wonderful happened: it became a part of me and began to sing, and I to sing through it. We gave each other a voice – one that sometimes hushed my teacher, whose fingers seemed clumsier than mine, though I was only eight.

"Oh, I think you have… *it*," he said.

Then added, "*I* don't. Not *really*," and smiled a little sadly.

"Yes, you do, Mr Lee!" I shouted. "We all love your songs in Assembly!" I meant it: he would bob and strum to the awful hymns, making them joyous and fun. We adored him, our Lord of the Dance.

Yet Mr Lee's private lessons never captured my heart as completely: songs like *Jimmy Crack Corn* and *Take Me Home, Country Roads* made me frown with boredom as I picked at the chords on my classical guitar, at its dark wood and black-plastic strings. They didn't sound like anything David Gilmour might play, I thought. How could I make a wondrous noise like he did? Or Ziggy the alien rockstar who chose me from the TV?

My sister's Spanish guitar wasn't as pretty as mine, but it chimed like an old church bell as I played a Bert Jansch piece she had learned at County School and taught me: all bronze strings and fading varnish. So, I borrowed hers and never gave it back. Naming the guitar made it mine, and hundreds of songs were hiding in Old Smokey's strings; I freed them, until the air seemed full of wings.

"What's wrong with *your* guitar?" asked my father, "it cost twenty pounds." "*That* is my guitar," I said, pointing at my absent sister's. "The other belongs to someone else." I believed it, and still do; guitars choose *you*, like wands. But in time, I discovered that what I really needed was a thing called a Stratocaster.

Then one day Mr Lee didn't turn up for my lunchtime lesson. This had never happened before, though he often lost track of hours and days. Like all teachers, he was overworked, exhausted, and underpaid, his sheen of idealism scratched and windworn like Old Smokey, middle age beckoning from undercrofts, from the sunken garden of time.

Aged nine now and indignant, I wandered off to find him, eventually spotting him in the staff room, asleep, a cigarette burned to ash in his stubby fingers. "You're *supposed* to be teaching me *guitar!*" I bellowed, pointing at him.

"How *dare* you come in here!" he shouted, startled awake with his Silk Cut. "Get out, boy! *Get out!*" And that was that (though I heard him sigh, "Oh… *damn it,*" as I ran away).

So, from that day onward, I vowed to teach myself – as I had done with everything else.

Mr Lee made music come to life, then handed me a future by showing me how to hold a guitar, tune it, and strum it – and to always do it with a twinkle. But in the end, it was his absence that taught me to make it my own: to discover the music within me, all moon-fingered and midnight blue.

Together we escaped, my guitar and me; and we've been running ever since. Down corridors, night streets, and dark halls of the mind.

From the world of disappointing men.

And from the people we really love.

Act Two

Owen's Arrow

What message would you send your younger self?

I don't remember precisely how long Owen and I were boyhood friends. Time is relative and memory fragile and unreliable. To a child, the school summer break is an endless vista of possibility, from which we return changed beyond recognition. But to someone middle-aged, it's just a brief interlude between Christmases.

We were ten, perhaps, and in each other's lives almost daily until our mid-teens, when Owen moved to the next town. In those far-off days of landlines, three-channel TV, pocket money, and no internet, that was like moving to Mars. But we made the journey a handful of times in the years that followed.

Nor do I recall exactly when we met, but I remember seeing him in his mum's garden, next door but one to ours: an intrepid looking boy with a track bike. He was half a year older than me: six months stronger, faster, and more confident.

Owen wore black school brogues with jeans that were too short for him, walked with his shoulders back, then stooped over his bike with a spanner. Here was a proper lad with business to attend to: oiling gears, painting out rust, or shooting at windows with his air rifle.

I wasn't a proper lad, not even close. I'd listen to *Good Morning, Starshine* and feel like Christmas inside.

I was playing outside, so it might have been a summer's day, screaming with swifts. They would shriek above Mrs Ward's garden next door, then wheel like fairground rockets above the giant poplar at the back of our house, later felled by the hurricane. The Dutch elm, my tree of ghosts, guarded the front until disease claimed it and left my family exposed to sunlight and strangers.

Or perhaps it was the morning after Bonfire Night, when I would prowl the long grass for spent fireworks – dark and wet as rolled, dirty dishcloths. Or was I looking for Jeremy, the patient frog who lived near the foot of our garden? His pond held real magick – flourishing life, though it was just weed and sticklebacks.

Whichever day it was in my eleventh year on Earth, I stood at the fence, knee-deep in hammock dust and ivy, until Owen noticed me. One of us might have thrown an old tennis ball at the other – over Mrs Ward's garden, a friendly grenade over No Man's Land. Or a Wham-o Frisbee, or an elastic-propelled rocket that spiralled to the ground on plastic-bag parachute. But most likely one of us just shouted, "Hey!"

You could do that, back then, win a friend with a word. And suddenly there he was: a hero. Armstrong to my Aldrin, Matt Mason to my Callisto. Owen scaled the wire fence into No Man's Land then dived over the second to stand at my side. Of course, we then had to hide: my parents might have seen me happy and intervened.

"*Wotcha!* Why are we in a bush?"
"*Shh*, you div! I'll explain later."
"Ay, you dress like a twat."
"Mohair. Mum knitted it."
"Shoes are cool, though."
"Converse!"
"Smart."

Owen, the poor boy, my old friend from the other side. The four houses in my parents' walled, private road (each garden taller than the next, so three could look down on their neighbours) existed in one universe. This was the cosmos of Mum and Dad, of big cars in the drive, independent school, freshly laundered clothes, and Sunday roasts. (The family at Number Four were a rum lot, though. Who could they look down on?)

But Owen lived in the other realm, the one my mother never wanted me to enter, let alone escape into – running, jumping, and laughing. He was the son of the caretaker of the County School for Girls, whose grand frontage – the school's, not the girls' – was a few hundred yards away, in acres of green and tennis courts. The caretaker's two-up, two-down cottage was in a corner of the grounds, making it our near neighbour.

I had made a working-class friend, and this horrified my mother. To make matters worse, we became inseparable;

Owen would come to the door almost daily and *actually ring the bell*. ("Why is that boy always here? What's *wrong* with him?" said Mum. "He's my friend and he *likes* me?" I ventured.)

It was an outrage from which she never quite recovered, though my friends became ever more varied over the years: rockers, misfits, punks, Indians, geeks, hippies, space cadets, girls in fur coats, drunks, queens, Northerners, Nigerians, indie boys, lovelorn men from record shops, and at least one psychopath. One day in my mid-teens, the Hell's Angels would turn up and nearly fall through the ceiling. (I'd befriended them by ordering a tequila sunrise during a police raid while my schoolfriends jumped out the pub window.)

Yet Owen's mum was a caretaker in every sense and accepted me without question. She was a warm, selfless woman doing back-breaking work to give her son a future, though he went to the rough school in the next town. She was a wise old girl, however; she could see the future when we could not. She knew that one day I would hurt her son, by getting on a train somewhere with books beneath my arm. She knew I would disappear.

His father had long ago vanished too; I don't think Owen ever knew his name. At one time a fancy man from the Norfolk Broads came calling for Owen's mum, but then drifted away. An older sister sometimes lurked in the cottage, but all love was lost between them.

So, my new friend's dad was missing, while mine was AWOL in the same room as his family. Both of us had sisters in the big world, and we both had mothers who had fallen prey to sadness: men were disappointing, daughters angry, and sons sapped women's strength while sometimes giving them hope. Though never quite enough.

Now Owen and I were *both* lost in space, entangled in some quantum state. But we were never weightless, not even for a moment. We found each other and shared a darkness, colliding and sparking each other back to life. I can see all this now, but back then neither of us spared a thought for gravity. I was clever and Owen was brave. There was a world to get lost in, and we did.

But first, we had to learn archery.

Take a bamboo pole, five feet long. Cut a slit in both ends with your rusty, pearl-handled penknife, then stretch a real bowstring between them. You now have a longbow that can bury a gold-tipped arrow – sharp in those days – in the bark of an ancient tree.

Or you can shoot your friend in the arm, as Owen did on the day I jumped out from behind an oak just as he loosed his string. "Sorry!" he shouted, running towards me in fright as I stood with the arrow in me, a gangly Saint Sebastian in anorak and trainers. We agreed never to mention him nearly killing me again.

We had quivers for our arrows and would run through the trees, hunting for sunlight. In a daydream, sometimes, I pictured the Spirit of Summer as a man made of flowers, wheat, ivy, and field corn – arms crossed, standing in the shadows for us to find him. A *māyā*, like Shakespeare's Herne with his ragg'd horns.

Or the Green Man of English folklore, the Green Knight to our Gawain and Galahad, a foliate spirit of the long days. Over the years, I've glimpsed him in my mind's eye, watching from the hedgerows as the sun arcs towards autumn. We are connected somehow, and he keeps me safe. Or perhaps I am haunted, under an Old English spell.

In the caretaker's shed, Owen built track bikes with handlebars like buffalo horns, while I stood astride the mule of my green Carlton racer. One day he said my hair looked cool – I'd grown it out that summer, the one with dead white lawns and the soundtrack of punk and tumbling skateboards.

He had given himself a buzzcut with clippers and told me I should touch it, because it felt like suede (Owen was always a factual friend). I did and, in that moment, we stood at the centre of the universe, he and I. I saw everything that had ever existed and would ever be, just for an instant. Then I snatched my hand away, dizzy. I felt part of things, connected, for the first time in my life: it was overwhelming.

But what did it mean? I knew, of course, deep down; yet far too deep to acknowledge, especially to myself.

Ours was the story of a million and one young people in those years – some gay, but most straight. Friends figuring out who they were in a world that didn't care but felt it should poke fun anyway. In those moments, Owen liked to work on his bike.

My mother was standing on a chair in the kitchen watching through binoculars as her errant son – always eccentric, sensitive, and strange – ran his fingers through another boy's hair. From that day onwards, she hated Owen with every atom of her being, pausing only to read her ballet magazines and admire the photos of Rudolph Nureyev and Robert Helpmann; she never saw the irony. (Every man my mother adored – dancer, actor, or TV star – seemed as gay as a window. And not just any window, but Liberty's at Christmas.)

We rode off into the far country then, Owen and me, to the isthmus between seasons. "Come on, let's go." "Where?" "Everywhere!" We found an air raid shelter that had never heard the Blitzkrieg. We climbed trees – I stopped halfway and watched him clamber to the top. We went swimming together, and hit grey balls at each other as Borg and Nastase – he the serious one, me the clown.

We sat on opposite sides of his room, nodding to *Brain Salad Surgery* by Emerson Lake and Palmer. *("You see, it really doesn't matter, when you're buried in disguise, by*

the dark glass on your eyes…") We never dared sit
together in that space, of course, though we would always
fight on the grass.

Out in the grounds, Owen would win our battles and look
at me, beaming. Only someone with crippling depression,
self-loathing, and dysmorphism could possibly understand
why this was important. In those moments, now lost in
time, I had made someone happy. This had never happened
before; I spent my youth surrounded by miserable, angry
people. Everywhere I looked there was sadness; it seeped
into your bones like damp.

"*Chris-to-pher…*" Owen would say, pulling a mock-sad
face, then throw back his head and laugh. We were sun and
moon; I reflected light back at him. I was alive at last, and
free. I had finally escaped the insanity of my parents: the
father who would click his fingers to summon me like a
dog, the mother who disapproved of everyone, especially
herself.

*– Now I was watched by the Spirit of Summer: his ancient
arms crossed in orchids and ivy. My horned guardian of
the green fields, his voice like the wind in dry grass.*

We had the run of the school at night, Owen and me. He
would steal his mum's keys and we'd roam the corridors
with torches as Starsky and Hutch. One night some of the
older girls were still there at an outbuilding disco. I
sneaked in and danced to The Real Thing with them in a
cloud of dry ice – danced as I had never done before, while

my best friend watched through the window (he wasn't allowed to mix with students). It was the first time I saw him look genuinely sad.

'To you I guess I'm just a clown, who picks you up each time you're down…'

My mother was a hundred yards away reading the Telegraph in the kitchen while her now teenaged son gyrated in the spotlight with fifty laughing sixth-form girls. Of course, she didn't see *that*.

But best of all, Owen and I had The Majestic. The old cinema, that Deco colossus, is now long gone. But this was where we gasped and fell silent at the mothership's arrival in *Close Encounters of the Third Kind*, sang along to the Pearl & Dean music, took notes in *Grease* and *The Slipper and the Rose*, yelled at the eyeless head in *Jaws*, cried with laughter at *Airplane!*, and scraped Blakeys on the seatbacks during *Pink Floyd Live at Pompeii*, passing Rothmans, Consulates, and Sobranie Black Russians down the line like joints.

We laughed ourselves hoarse at *Monty Python and the Holy Grail* ("Someday, lad, all of this will be yours…" "What, *the curtains*?"). We saw *Star Wars* together, Owen and me, as if summoned by the Force. And we were the only audience in the huge theatre for *Logan's Run*, a story about people who are not allowed to grow old.

Much later we sneaked into *Caligula*, uncensored, and Ken Russell's *Altered States*, an education neither of us were quite ready for. The adult world we were joining felt remote, dangerous, and impenetrable. Because it was. I knew that better than anyone.

But long before then, something happened to change everything. One winter's night at the Majestic when I was almost fourteen, a girl – an actual girl! – came between us. Her name was Philippa, and we caught each other's eye while I was at the Kia Ora stand buying sweets and a bag of Butterkist.

The words I said to her worked ("Do you want my sherbert dib-dab?"), though I was looking good in my cheesecloth shirt and Chucks; still recognisably Clix, my boyhood self. This was in the months before adolescence disfigured me and made me a stranger to everyone, especially myself. It was before the sadness came and stayed forever.

It was brave of me to approach her, though with short hair, flat chest, and turned-up nose, she looked reassuringly gamine. And so it was, on that dark day in my fourteenth year as a simpleton, Philippa – clever, warm, and freckled with humour – walked back to the seats with me and sat between Owen and myself.

Weeks later she would send me a Christmas card with the words 'All my love, Phil xxx' scribbled in biro. Thank God there was just enough space for me to add '-ippa' to her name and avert another crisis for my mother.

But now, in the permanent dusk of The Majestic, lit by storm-flashes of movie magick, something awful was happening as I sat with my arm around her shoulder, feeling almost – but not quite – like a real boy at last. Looking to my left, past Philippa's smiling face and lips ready for a kiss (I obliged), I saw something that opened a portal to the future.

What I saw told me I would blunder through life for over a decade more until, one day in my late twenties, I would finally lock eyes with my own in the shaving mirror and shout, "Wake *up*, Chris! Stop lying to yourself. You're a gay man, you're a fucking poof. You fancy men, and you always have. Just deal with it. *Everyone knows.*"

But back in '77, Owen – the boy who could mend anything, my hero, and my best friend – was staring right at me as I sat with my arm around Philippa. And he was… *crying.*

– Owen never cried, I thought. He was a proper lad in a bomber jacket and checked shirt. Had something happened? Did I miss something in the film?

Our friendship limped on for a few years afterwards, but something seemed broken now, deep down; something neither of us understood, or could put into words. We lived in a small, Conservative town in the 1970s and Eighties, a world of silence and kept appearances.

It was a place where our local MP would drive around playing *Land of Hope and Glory* through a megaphone, to the dullest people imaginable. There was nothing to do but drink and try to jump over hedges, or watch Dick Emery on TV wearing a handbag and makeup for laughs.

Owen and I would still collide occasionally over the years, go out sometimes, or catch a movie; but when he moved away the phone calls became fewer. Until one day there was just the dialling tone and the receiver put back, gently but decisively.

Click.

Then one morning in 2010, staring out to sea from my window, I decided to track him down for old times' sake. A moment of madness, no doubt; but relativity was calling again.

There was no trace of my old friend on the internet, except a sole directory listing for someone of the same name, just a couple of miles from where we grew up. (The distance had seemed so insurmountable and traitorous back then, but sun and moon were neighbours all along.) The estimated age was right and listed as a former co-occupant of the address was a woman, a name that died out after the war. (I could feel his mother's wise, sad eyes looking at me across the decades. She was shaking her head.)

I wrote a letter to this possible stranger, but probable long-lost best friend, apparently now living alone. As I typed I found myself picturing Owen the last time I saw him as a grown-up, and that moment years earlier when Philippa had sat between us, sucking on a Kia Ora; his sadness in the strobing screen-light of *The Island of Doctor Moreau*. They seemed like messages from the distant past. Or so I thought.

I apologised for writing, so he would know it was me. I said I regretted sometimes pushing him away when he had phoned back then, inviting me out in the car he'd built from a wreck to see the flying machines he knew I loved. (Mum standing over me, telling me to put the receiver down.)

I said I was sorry, more than I could say, that I had blanked him one day in the early Nineties, when he stood staring at me and another friend. Owen was smiling, waiting for me to acknowledge him. It was our last encounter...

It was a summer's day and I had walked across the park to The Castle pub with an old friend, listening to 'Loveless' by My Bloody Valentine on my Walkman. Suddenly there he was again, in that magickal way of his: Owen, standing at the bar with a pint, now a handsome man in his twenties (my heart skipped a beat). We saw each other and froze. But something made me look away.

What was it, I wonder? Too much gravity, perhaps. I have regretted it ever since.

In the letter I explained that, back in the day, he had knocked around with an idiot. I told him what a wonderful friend he had been, that I had a million happy memories of our times together. And finally, I said that if he was ever in town, he should look me up and I'd finally buy him that drink. We'd set the world to rights again, him and me.

'Stupid fish, I drank the pool', as Colin Blunstone once sang.

Even today when I'm downstairs picking up the post, I sometimes slip my hand into the mailbox and feel for the reply I know will never come. On cold mornings I feel Owen's arrow in my arm, a twinge of ancient pain. But my old friend is never coming back.

And it's fine, I understand. Too many years have passed – a lifetime, in fact; it was a mistake even to write. For all I know, Owen has forgotten me completely, and who could blame him? Plus, we are in the shadows now, where once we ran.

Maybe I wanted to right a distant wrong, edit my past, correct a stupid mistake, and let Owen know that I had always treasured the years we spent together. Or perhaps I wanted to give my younger self the gift of sight, so Clix, laughing boy that I was, could see what was right before his idiot eyes: someone who actually cared.

– To drop a bottle in the sea of time and watch it drift away, back through that portal to the Majestic cinema in 1977, to the island of our impossible pasts.

So, what would I tell my younger self?

Washed up onshore, my message to Clix would tell him to say the one thing to Owen that he never could back then, but really should have. And quickly, before it was too late. That thing he really *wanted* to say, but hostile times, guilt, and shame had always swept away – again and again.

To grab his friend and say, "*I love you*, you div. But I'm frightened."

Bookends

THE ROAD RIDER FOUR
(A song about skateboards)

Got my Henry Hester board
Got my gold Gull Wings
Got my Road Rider Fours,
ruby risers and Sims

Mitch got a Surf Flier deck,
Russ wants a Logan Earth Ski
Down that dusty old ridge,
where the summer's hid

at Skate City

And Owen says…
Boys don't you move so fast
You might fall on your knees
He rides an old Tomahawk
and wears brogues with his jeans

So, we wait for him.

(song written as christopher rye)

Act Three

The Woman Who Stayed

"Hello? It's only me…"

Photos of Mary Bryant from the 1940s and Fifties reveal a glamorous young woman of almost Latin beauty: raven hair, high cheekbones, strong brows, and a confident smile.

In one she is standing chic and demure in a Chelsea doorway. In another, she sits happily on a beach somewhere, surrounded by handsome admirers. In a third, she is radiant, slim, and laughing on a Kensington rooftop, hair thrown back in the summer breeze.

I would love to have known that woman: she seemed warm, confident, fun, ambitious. (Elegant but understated, a petite French bonnet and an Italian coat, a touch of Chanel or Mitsouko.) Years earlier, she had dodged Hitler's doodlebugs and sheltered in tube stations while London shook and burned.

Mary had seen tragedy by then. Born at the end of the First World War, she had lost twin brothers to the flu pandemic, grown up in the Great Depression, lost her father in her teens, and her mother as a young woman. Then she used an inheritance to set herself up in the capital, where she entered the Civil Service. But the second war came, bringing with it a career in the War Office. In a sense, she never left it: our family was always on a battlefield.

But by late middle age, Mary had become a very different person: overweight and unrecognisable from those carefree post-war images. Often, she was severe, belligerent, suspicious, and prejudiced. As Mary Middleton, she lost all interest in herself, her ulcered legs bandaged beneath thick beige stockings, the legacy of late motherhood.

Mum claimed I had healing hands as a little boy, that I gave her life in return. It was a beautiful thing to say; but all that changed in my teens.

Mum was nearly fifty when I was born. By then, she was desperately lonely and, according to my aunt, had long been planning her escape from Dad. (She told her, "All I wanted was a companion, but instead I have a man who never talks to me.") She had no friends locally, no social circle; her international world had shrunk to a kitchen in a loveless house. In time, it began to drive her mad.

Mary had married a man she should have run from, yet would stay at his side for over half a century. This was the woman who had once boarded propellor planes alone with her passport half open like tiny wings. She had walked the lanes of Florence and Versailles, gazed from her Whitehall window at the King's funeral cortege, arranged international conferences, edited journals, seen Fonteyn and Nureyev dance, and sat in the Royal Opera House with Nikita Khrushchev.

– Oh, the light summer dresses, they circled and bobbed, and the hummingbird embroidered a kiss in the lily…

Family legend has it that my parents slept together only twice, seven years apart, making my sister and me. Doubtless that was true. But why have a second child if she was about to run? Was I forced on Mum to stop her, as punishment for defying her husband?

It would explain a great deal, such as the time she rolled her eyes in horror at a mention of sex. "*Disgusting business,*" she muttered, tearfully. She claimed to hate parties, drinks, and social gatherings too, though Mary Bryant's photos said otherwise.

Or perhaps the shame of divorce, of becoming a middle-aged spinster – with no income of her own – persuaded her to stay. Or was I Mum's escape from loneliness, her solution to it, giving her daughter a young companion? A little brother for a gift, almost wrapped in a bow.

(Joanna and I remain close to this day, and share blissful memories of listening to albums and radio plays together – *Teaser and the Firecat*, *Bridge Over Troubled Water*, and *The Hitchhiker's Guide to the Galaxy* – of dressing up, speaking in silly voices, and giggling. We went to gigs and shopped for hippy clothes, and I'd act out *The Boxer* and *The Only Living Boy in New York* to make her laugh. Or *Say You Don't Mind* by Colin Blunstone, *Catch the Wind* by Donovan, and *The Days of Pearly Spencer*. But then she vanished to university, and afterwards to Scotland, leaving me in the ghostship of the family home.)

– One day I was a gift again, only this time to strangers.
But all that is to come, much later in my story.

Mary Bryant had been a modern, independent woman
before she met my father, then married him when she was
turning forty. Oh, she should have run. I have a photo of
Mum in the kitchen in Folkestone, with a garden bird in her
hand. She is holding it to the window so it can fly away…

She was indomitable, though. Life with Dad had drained
her of hope, but not of fight. In all the decades I knew her,
she was ill in bed for just a single day.

My father admired strong, outspoken women, but hadn't
intended to marry one, it seems. This was Mum's tragedy.
She gave up her independence, life in London, travel, and a
career for him. ('*In every dream home a heartache*', as
Roxy Music sang.) She was far from alone among women
of her generation, of course.

She called Dad 'Middleton', but I don't remember him ever
calling her Mary. To him, she was nameless, and this left
her with a simmering pain. In more than half a century
together, I don't recall my father ever complimenting her,
thanking her for anything, asking her opinion, or even just
having a conversation with her.

In his on/off romance with the binary world, Dad was
number one, and Mum was zero. He belittled her, talked
down to her, and wore her away with a million tiny

absences. In turn, she fought back and enraged him. This was the case long before I was born.

The pattern was loud and endlessly repeating, like 1970s wallpaper: hours of silence followed by some *fait accompli* from Dad that Mum disapproved of – a Heath Robinson addition to the house, no doubt, heralded by hours of hammering and sawing. Then the shouting and screaming began; I never understood why they couldn't just talk. On one occasion, she threatened him with an axe. This was how the other half lived in Surrey towns.

But my mother was eccentric in her own way too; often wonderfully so. Like most Whitehall people, she would cry with laughter at dirty jokes – the filthier the better – but sounded disconcertingly like the Queen.

She would invent words ("I'm going for a fuddle around the shops") and mispronounce others. Mum swore the word 'unstable' (which she had cause to use often) rhymed with 'Dunstable' ("I think your father may be *un*stubble, Christopher!"). One day at the seaside, she announced, "I love a good stiff blow on the front!" causing me to collapse in helpless giggles. "My mother was the same," she added. Her imperiousness made it funnier, yet she was always baffled by my laughter.

But at times of crisis, Mum had no idea what to say. The day my tearful aunt rang to say she had found my much-adored uncle dead in his armchair, Mum thought hard for a second and said, "It must have been something *terrible* he ate."

In such moments of blackest comedy, I often despaired. How could someone who had lived through Depression, war, and personal tragedy – who had heard the engines of flying bombs cut out, seen streets destroyed, and watched sightless, shell-shocked men grope for their former lives – have so little talent with people?

Years later when my aunt was fading too and in her final bed, Mum sat in the other room staring into space, unable to think of a single thing to tell her sister. (I sat with my aunt, put my arm around her shoulder, and told her I loved her. God knows, it wasn't hard.)

Even by the 1970s, my parents were afflicted by the relativity of late middle age. For them, silences passed quickly, but for me in the slow, candescent plume of childhood, they lasted for years.

I was born into a world of computers, Concorde, space rockets, and pop radio – of *Fab 208*, Radio Luxembourg, Emperor Rosko, and John Peel – while Mum and Dad were the age of my schoolfriends' grandparents. For them, coming of age had meant the Blitz and young men in trenches, but for me in the early Eighties it would mean the Blitz Kids and young men in trench coats and eyeliner.

– Danny's father was barely forty even then. Years earlier, he had left his toddler son on the bar at the UFO Club

*while he rolled in lysergic jelly and danced to Syd
Barrett's Pink Floyd. But for my pensioner mother,
Rowntree's jelly was an adventure.*

I must have seemed alien to my war-torn parents, like
Thomas Jerome Newton in *The Man Who Fell to Earth*;
certainly, I felt that way. Or Edward Scissorhands, the
unfinished boy sitting alone in the dark house, cutting
things into pretty shapes. (Or sewing sequins onto felt, as I
was taught to do at middle school when Mum refused to let
me learn about sex: useful training for a glamourous gay
man.)

"*There*," she said, slipping her latest creation over my
Adidas t-shirt, as I stood, aged ten, in my favourite Levi's
and Converse. "Now you look like a *real* man. One day
you'll be an Army officer!" It was an orange, tiger-striped
mohair tank top (she had knitted a lilac one as a spare).
"Now run along," she chirped. "But don't talk to the new
people at the school. They're not our sort *at all*." Thank
God I didn't listen.

But as I grew up, the black comedy stopped, and a present
darkness, coldness, and anger descended on her: a Joan
Crawford-style bitterness that could be alarming and
forbidding. Homophobia was part of it, but there was
something deeper and more sequestered too. It was the
memory of something, perhaps, as though this once warm
and nurturing woman was haunted by something terrible
and unspoken.

– What was it? I wonder.

In those moments, she would tell me I was "an insignificant boy", that no one would ever pay attention to me, or even look at me. This was a bitter woman projecting, someone whose dream of life with a romantic, attentive man had proved to be an illusion. I had stopped Mum from leaving simply by being alive. *"You're still young, that's your fault,"* as Cat Stevens sang.

An insignificant boy... I can almost, in the outer reaches of my imagination, conceive of saying such a thing once in anger, then regretting it and apologising. But between the ages of thirteen and fifteen, when any boy is vulnerable, she sat me down and methodically, repeatedly, used those words to dismantle what little of my self-confidence adolescence and a repressive private senior school hadn't already destroyed. (But at least she remembered I existed: there's always an upside.)

By now Mum's sadness, which had once been love, knew no bounds. She had once been a warm, smiling presence who taught me to read and write before I was four, who sat at the old upright piano with me as I picked out the melody that made her smile – my tiny feet never reaching the pedals. We were devoted to each other, then; she gave me every advantage I had in life.

One day my father destroyed the piano with a sledgehammer, in one of those explosions of rage that seemed coded into his being. He would seethe, fume, mourn, and curse, even when alone. *What else might such a man be capable of?* I would find out one day, and perhaps Mum already had.

But for now, he would rail at his own mistakes: an imperfectly drawn line, an inkblot, a missed key on his manual typewriter. Any action less perfect than a theorem would make him sob in torment, lamenting his own imperfection. This enigma who would walk on the edges of kerbs, like Charles Blondin on a tightrope, but invariably stumble into the road. This man of constant sorrow, of limitless self-regard – and bottomless self-hatred.

– As Danny would later observe, I was living in a madhouse.

Above all, Dad wanted quiet in his glorious domain, the silence of a cosmos hurtling towards entropy. But in later years I brought rock music, discord, laughter, and parties to it. And a voice that spoke up for itself, always. We get the children we deserve; I learned to defy him, to challenge him, to state my case, and to always be slightly late – to live in sweet imperfection under his strict rule.

But with Mum, fighting back was harder, because I felt sorry for her. I didn't want to be my father's echo, just another man shouting at a depressed woman – though in the end that's exactly what happened, as she became evermore right wing and intolerant of her own children. She thought the Daily Mail a "left-wing rag"; this was the era of Margaret Thatcher, that sinecure for the privileged, lost, rich, and angry.

Mum's loneliness left her with a paranoid interest in our non-existent private lives; an obsession that, at times, was prurient, dark, and disturbing for my sister and me: eavesdropping on our phone calls, sniffing our dirty clothes, and accusing us of being whores.

What had happened to this woman to make her so full of bitterness, so disgusted at normal life? One can only speculate. At moments in my teens, I thought her completely insane. Or was she trying to protect us? From something – or someone?

With Dad's affection withdrawn from her, Mum measured out her life in teaspoons, in the *Telegraph* and the *Dancing Times*, in the laundry and ironing, in the tulip bulbs she planted, in rhododendron buds and magnolia trees, and in her daily trips to the supermarket with wicker basket and headscarf.

I'll Follow the Sun played in the desolate kitchen, then *The Navy Lark*, *Round the Horne*, Jimmy Young, and *The Clitheroe Kid:* Mum's radio held the world in its leatherette box.

Coffee at eleven, *Woman's Hour* at two, warm the pot for tea at ten to four, then prepare dinner for seven o'clock. Finally, the dishes before bed. This was the sum of a woman's loneliness. And it was the story of millions of invisible, unappreciated women in a world of distant, misogynistic men: dusting, ironing, folding, tidying, then sat alone at the kitchen table, disappearing to Radio Four.

– Knitting her absence into colourful clothes, as the radio reassured and comforted, while the paper warned of socialists under the bed.

Yet even in our difficult years, Mum loved to meet my schoolfriends. She had names for them all and would glimmer in the hallway with cups of tea until Mary was visible again, just for a second. They loved her. In those moments, I did too.

Though she later rejected me, Mum's love for her queer son would remain in secret, slipping me £20 notes and whispering *"Don't tell your father."* Like the little river that ran beneath Reigate, it flowed in darkness – in the caves below the shoe shops and manicured gardens, under the back alleys and overgrown paths, only breaking surface in bad weather.

But when Mum and Dad finally moved from the old house in the mid-1990s (I had long escaped to London), it became obvious she was suffering from dementia. Dad had never noticed, because forty years of routine had hidden it from him – from all of us, though she would often tell the same stories again and again.

Such as the time she saw train robber Ronnie Biggs in Folkestone after his escape from prison in 1965. He winked at her after emerging from a phone box, then ran towards the harbour while I was lying in my pram[11]. Was it true? Perhaps. But Mum also believed she had married a romantic, that her son just hadn't met the right girl.

Mum's daily routine became her memory – until the routine stopped; then she was lost forever. In her twilight years, she would look at paintings of country houses she had never visited and remember living in them: gazing from their windows, fields waving with grass that might tease a sleeping lover, dark poppies attended by bees. A Passchendaele of the mind and heart.

– *Her long gown a presage, musty and eternal, where childhood hides like a thief of lilies and stars.*

When Mum passed away in late 2013, at the age of ninety-five – in a flat next door to a schoolfriend of hers, whom Dad forbade her to see – I visited my father after years of estrangement. I thought it the right thing to do, to reach out to someone I imagined was in pain. But he suddenly told me how much he missed my aunt, who had died twenty years earlier – the aunt who looked like Ingrid Bergman; my rock and emotional support as a boy.

"I *loved* her," he said, but didn't say a word about the woman he had spent over half a century with. Had he married Mum to be closer to her sister, the wife of his only friend? I was dumbstruck, but this was hardly a new experience. The ability of this irascible yet eerily polite man to shock and confound was undimmed.

I left, and never looked back.

****

When Mum died, I had just bought a piano, the first I had ever owned. It arrived packed flat, so I had to put it together myself. As I sat on the floor with the pieces around me, I realised I was reassembling the smashed instrument from my early childhood – only a white one, like its ghost. A spectre.

Though she and I had not spoken for years, I wrote a classical piece on it, based on the melody I would play for her at the age of four. I named it *Black Swan*, honouring the person Mum had been before the loneliness set in; the beautiful young woman who had smiled in the dark as Garbo laughed and Nureyev danced. A woman I had never met.

At her funeral, Dad gave strict instructions that no one was to write tributes, give readings, or do anything that expressed emotion at her loss: he wanted silence, of course: a swift, orderly cremation, and nothing more. *Put her in the ground and move on*.

My sister and I ignored him and told Mum's life story, read poetry she loved, shared her favourite ballet music, and a recording of *Black Swan* played over the PA – everyone told me how beautiful it was. Better still, the church was full of African mourners: a wonderful fuck-you.

Dad sat hissing like a viper, cursing our defiance – at his own wife's funeral – incensed that the last word was not his. Mum would not be silenced in life, and neither would we in her memory; though she had taken out her bitterness on both of us, my sister and me.

Yet in the near-empty diaries he left after his own death – alone in the wilds of Oxfordshire, miles from family – the anniversary of Mum's passing was always marked in black. The same spidery, italic hand that had once sent her poetry.

By this time, Dad had one chair, one table, and kept his clothes in a filing cabinet, beneath a solar system made from coffee-tin lids nailed to the wall. In his final days he took to throwing himself out of bed and dragging himself towards his cosmos. Refusing the help of a black carer.

Then at last his madness was over, and the universe reclaimed him.

****

Some years before Mum's passing, on the last occasion I spent time with her alone, I arranged for her to stand on the Royal Opera House stage after the audience had left; it was a production of *Romeo and Juliet*.

Mum had taken to going to the ballet again on her own, just as she had done in the 1950s before she met my father: nodding in the dark as the dancers leapt and spun, an echo of her former life.

John, a gay friend of mine who worked in the crush bar, took us down in a hidden lift from the amphitheatre – she had no idea of the surprise until we led her onstage. Then we raised the curtain and Mum curtsied in the spotlight to tumultuous silence, though by then she could barely walk. *"Thank you,"* she said to me. Then looked away, adding, "Your friend is very nice..."

Perhaps I knew, deep down, that I was saying goodbye to her that day; by giving her a long-cherished dream, by letting Mary Bryant tread the boards so I could finally meet her.

Onstage, Mum saw the chipboard scenery up close – it had seemed so beautiful from the gods – while I read the bitchy gay graffiti on the back of it and chuckled to myself: jokes about the sexual talents of the male stars she worshipped, scrawled in black paint and marker pen all across the rear of the wooden flats. (I lacked the cruelty to show it to her, tempting though it was.)

We see what we need to see: Juliet's bedroom, or a camp illusion; the set for an ancient dance.

But there she was, at last.

Mary Bryant, smiling.

Bookends

Holidays with Joanna

I am lying in the womb of the sea, where the moon, curled as if unborn, pushes until her waters break along the shore.

"Ocean, since my time began, I have troubled your waters returning home. I know the waves flow through every man. I am no different, only raised up and cast afloat before your eyes…" on my midnight blue Lilo, writing poems in my head.

On Folkestone Leas, down the Zig-Zag Path to a big ship that holds the horizon, a distant boat train curved along the harbour wall. The tea shop is "quite pleasant", says Mum, though it took an hour to choose it beneath a clamour of gulls. We roll our eyes and giggle.

Beyond the cathedral, the castle, the ancient stone circle, we walk in threes or twos, but never as a four. Another stately home to be quiet in, yearning for dodgems and candy floss. Giggling on the top deck, bouncing over the bumps.

– And the long, slim fish that Owen caught with beautiful uncertainty. Turning, he said something to the evening light and waited for hope to harden his face. While I, untying lover's knots, tinderbox-painted a sunset with the sparks of stars, my sense of wonder tempered and

reconciled. Then I stood with a gorse bush framing my face
and watched the smoke-pale butterflies.

At Prussia Cove, we laugh among the lobster pots, Joanna
and me. Ribena fizzes in chalky water as we clamber back
from the beach. Moths tick against the lamp in the
tumbledown stone cottage. There is sand in my shorts.

"When the ships are dark, the lighthouse keeper comes
home from the ocean, trailing its stars, his icy hand tight
on the back door..."

To Scotland to see her: searching for monsters in Loch
Ness, tilting on the riding sea in Oban Bay, tiny rainbows
o'er the rocks at the Isle of Skye, where narrow paths lift
wheels into hollows, ending with roads. We shout against
the wind in our rain-lashed kagoules.

On Boxing Day, melodies of footprints climb through the
frost as our snowman wilts in Aunty's garden. (The French
film about the missing shoe: we laugh until it hurts,
gorging ourselves sick on marzipan and chocolate shells.)

– And the ancient cross on the Normandy hillside,
and the circling streets of Mont Saint-Michel.
And Miss Legg dancing at a Quinéville disco,
and the seesaw in the dusty square.
And the crab on a tea plate that made Andrew puke,
and the train to Paris that rainy dawn.
And the waiter who was female too...
and our gossip in the dusty dorm.

And Omaha, Utah, Juno, and Sword,
and the landing craft blown east by storm.
And the rock I threw just to make a splash,
but David lay broken in teacher's arms.
Then he won a race, laughing, and waved at me,
so I cried with joy as he sped past... [12]

Reading *Now We Are Six* on our parents' bed as the Sixties pass over Reigate Hill. The Seventies glimmer with power cuts, clogs, and patchwork bags, with fluorescent toys beneath the bedclothes. The dip-flash of Uncle's headlights on a dark country road, white lines strobing behind us like tracer.

At Shanklin, a handsome man carries us across the waves in our espadrilles, to the pedalo where we dub him 'Sir Galahad'.

We loom above the model village, my sister and me. We are bigger than this little town.

There are things I want to tell her. But I can't.

Act Four

The Boy in the Thorns

(How my life was torn apart)

If time ran backwards, we would back away from memory.

"And NOW, ladies and gentlemen, for your delight and delectation, the Mixed-Up Radio Show PRESENTS...!"

1974, aged ten. Waiting in the wings of my middle-school's end-of-term show, I tell my group of whispering, giggling friends to pick me up and throw me onto the stage, so I arrive in a crash of flailing limbs as the audience laughs. I know how to make an entrance – onstage, at least; in life I am already less certain.

My friends march on behind me as a barbershop choir, with clip-on moustaches and towels. I dust myself down, straighten the tie that reaches my knees, and begin waving my arms with gusto.

The choir sings in cod-manly voices: *"On the fourth day of Christmas my true love gave to me: four Dorking perms, three French men, two rubber gloves, and an artist with a bare knee...!"* I hadn't told the school I had written new words.

At *"FIVE... OLD... QUEENS...!"* the headmaster's face turns pink with rage (I had thought the phrase referred to ancient monarchs). Miss Anthony's head is buried in her hands, but her shoulders are shaking. Then she looks up, beams at me, and pats the headmaster's knee – very gently.

"It's *Christmas*," I see her say, gesturing at the cheering, laughing pupils. "And look, they *love* him." He smiles weakly and begins clapping along.

Kenneth Williams, Spike Milligan, Bob Newhart, Abbott and Costello, Monty Python, Laurel and Hardy, Dave Allen, Jerry Lewis, and Kenny Everett's anarchic radio shows… I stole from them all and fashioned a camp, surreal, madcap comedy of my own that played with words and hidden meanings.

As Clix, I wrote sketches and plays, and acted them out in English lessons. I told stories, and experimented with tape loops, transmitters, and cathode ray tubes. Yet I was anything but a difficult boy; I knew to give my parents the space their misery demanded. In return, they left me solitary, bereft, and unencouraged.

Yet I was so happy in those years: often alone, but never lonely. There was always something to do, make, or discover. There still is.

Photos of me from those early years show a wide-eyed and quietly confident child – one who taught himself to swim in five minutes, after years of being screamed at in swimming pools. A boy who felt sorry for a goalkeeper once, so kicked the ball into his hands. A joker who talked too much in class, perhaps, but only because he found himself among *people* for the first time, rather than trapped in odd, Edwardian seclusion at home – ever lost behind the tree of ghosts.

"He's here again!" I would announce when I stomped into the room as a toddler, parroting my mother's words. I learned detachment early, even from myself.

Here was a space-boy with his mind on the stars, but a generational gulf at his shoulder. A clown who would stick a putty eyepatch to his face then limp into the classroom as Quasimodo for his latest drama production. A boffin who showed other pupils how radio waves and electricity worked, making things explode in the middle-school science lab.

A child who was popular, bright, and happy – for a while. A storyteller more than a show-off, his brain fizzing with ideas, as the roiling sea once hushed the pebbles on Folkestone beach.

– He's here again: the child with the man in his eyes. And the Spirit of Summer smiles from the hedgerow, his noble arms crossed in lilies and wild grasses; the benign wraith I conjured to keep me safe.

Ah, where did you go, old friend? Why did you let it happen?

Clix lived in big houses, private roads, and beautiful gardens. I never wanted for possessions, though I did want for love, encouragement, and support. I had heat, light, and gadgets to play with, most of which I built myself. I had a room of my own, a den in which to invent a future and a purpose. I had both my parents – for better or worse – plus some wonderful, loyal friends. And I had comfort, if not quite security: like Tom in his *Midnight Garden* as the clock struck thirteen.

But strike thirteen it did.

I didn't grow up in a warzone, though I dwelt in the memory of one. I didn't live in poverty, or on a sink estate full of dealers and gangs. I never had to carry a gun or knife – though later considered both in my darker moments. I was white, male, middle-class, and well educated: born by the sea and living in the Home Counties. More, I was talented and clever, writing poetry in my head beneath a sky full of swifts.

So why, by the age of eighteen, had I become a withdrawn, frightened wreck, barely able to communicate or look people in the eye?

I will tell you.

– "D-D-Dan," I said. *"Help me."*

*****

"Autumn evenings made me who I am. In the hush of falling leaves, you'll find the man." ('Thunderstorms', a song I wrote as a boy.)

I didn't break down less than twenty-four hours after leaving senior school because I was shy, nervous, or weak; I have never been any of those things, though in my teens and twenties I doubtless appeared that way to insecure men. And they were everywhere.

My breakdown and slow recovery in the years that followed was a form of post-traumatic stress, a string snapping that had been stretched too tightly across seven violent, horrific years at senior school. But above all, it was because a demon was now playing my tune; one I'd encountered many years before, then tried to forget.

– You will meet it soon. For me, it came as a memory.

I hung onto Clix, my boyhood self, for as long as I could: his restless imagination, creativity, and good humour. It helped that for my first fourteen years of life I had the looks my mother once had: I was fine featured, dark haired, blue-eyed, and always laughing: a brazen, pretty boy who old ladies would smile at in the supermarket.

In my mid-teens, that childhood version of me became a wellspring of hope and optimism that kept me going. But Clix himself disappeared.

You could say I used him up to survive, and in the process became a completely different soul: an odd, moonlit youth with a guitar, who tuned into the stories and melodies in his head. Like my Magnavox radio at night, always searching for a signal; or my Stellaphone tape recorder, wearing out an old reel until it came apart in my fingers.

A young man who wrote five hundred songs, recorded them himself – playing all the instruments – then put the tapes in a drawer and slammed it shut. I no longer wanted to be seen or heard.

The candle I had long held as a boy guttered, leaving me with nothing but dancing shadows. To the outside world, the frail, damaged creature I became in my teens and early twenties must have been a mystery. A puzzle wrapped in a midnight jacket.

Before then, I could talk to girls long before my friends plucked up the courage to. Perhaps the fact I was secretly gay – albeit locked in a Narnia of closets – made me seem confident to female friends, because I had no fear of rejection. (Unlike my weird friend PJ, who shouted *"Extending! Extending!"* on his own in the changing rooms the day he discovered his erection.)

At parties, girls would smile at the boyhood version of me then stare at the floor while playing with their hair. Clix had a string of female admirers, such as Lois, the glamorous older girl next door; Barbara, the Farah Fawcett of junior school; Victoria, my aunt's horsey neighbour; Philippa, of course; and J, the witchy goth at my palatial middle school.

It was an 18th Century priory set in acres of beautiful parkland. There I was actor, musician, playwright, TV cameraman, and comedian. A happy child in a welcoming, progressive, wealthy school.

J was a dark combination of Stevie Nicks and Siouxsie Sioux. She would throw wild, bat-themed parties, and dance like a dervish in black taffeta and top hat. Years later, she was arrested for gun running.

But then fate played a joke on me, and everything changed. It began, innocuously enough, when puberty hit me like a Biblical plague when I was fourteen, at my grim, decaying senior school – a Dickensian throwback full of violence, predation, rugby, and oppression. In that Victorian hellhole of dark sarcasm and lingering threat, I had a thousand boys' acne for them so they could have clear skin. Soon, that private school became my public hell.

Clix, a boy once handsome enough to be cooed over in sweetshops, pounding the streets in his Converse sneakers, sucking on Space Dust, and riding his board... he vanished one day and was replaced by an interloper: a stretched, misshapen, sullen adolescent. An angular, bullied youth who shot up six inches in as many months without putting on an ounce of weight.

Teenagers live in an eternal present, so none of my classmates remembered that I had once been one of the best-looking boys in school. Now, I had always been ugly, a freak; the idea that I had once been anything else – distant months before – was absurd.

I was beaten up in tunnels, kicked to the floor at the end of lessons, and buried under piles of chairs, but was now too physically frail to respond with anything but sarcasm. One day while walking home I was pelted with rocks, mud, and stones, like a leper.

Of course, this was just an extreme form of adolescence: grim, debilitating, and difficult, but hardly unique. Just the everyday nightmare of being a teenager: of changing and growing up different, though my results spiralled to earth with depression.

But it was merely the surface of my problems, what people *imagined* I was sad about. The reality was far deeper than finding myself skinny, big featured, and with bad skin. I was starting to remember something that had happened years before. And that memory – long repressed – was now unpicking my life and my boundless sense of hope.

– My dark daydream of the shadow in the trees had returned. Only now I understood its meaning, as puberty filled in the blanks. (But deep down, I had always known.)

I became a Rothko in a world of Kandinskys. A teenager whose mother mistook depression for drug use and rifled through his things daily in search of syringes and powders, finding only notebooks of poems, stories, and songs;

private thoughts that she used against him. They vanished from my room, leaving me both exposed and hidden.

To the day she died, Mum believed I was a junkie, based on nothing but my catatonia and withdrawal in my teens. She ignored my eventual breakdown ("Do you want to spend the rest of your life in a *hospital*?!" she shouted above the dishes one day), while my father chased his visage among the stars. A silence that revealed more than anyone knew.

And so, my seven years at senior school became the Seven Circles of Hell, with no respite at all at home. For four of those years, I was marked absent every day: I stopped going to Assembly and went for long walks on my own instead, daily before lessons began. Despite my efforts, I was never expelled. They just... gave up on me.

– *I was disappearing, fading from the world.*

Lateness gave me power, rebellion, and a moment's tranquillity; a vanishing space in which I could be myself. This wasn't self-importance, but the opposite: a terror of being seen. Clix had become an 'X' in the register rather than a tick.

One day my watch was wrong, so I turned up on time by accident: the entire school jeered and whistled when I walked into the hall, a far cry from the days when all my middle-school friends would cheer.

On my eighteenth birthday I staggered to school drunk at 9am, then sat giggling at clouds after a magic mushroom breakfast (a one-off gift from a friend). At a school concert later that year I left my guitar feeding back on the empty stage, screaming, while I sat in the graveyard smoking. At least the dead didn't judge me. Not for refusing to perform anyway.

The problem was I was disintegrating on the *inside*, where previously I had been so strong. This was because of something that no one knew except me. The storm of physical and emotional violence in which I found myself, at home and at school, had begun to trigger flashbacks to events from early boyhood. Things I had long shut away.

I was haunted by horrors that crept from my subconscious. Images of strangers and thorns, of a violent assault and a bloody rose. The man in the trees again, and an owl with its back turned. *But what were they?* Deep down, I always knew. I just couldn't face the truth.

Then the demon came, into the emptiness that fate had prepared for it. That was when I finally accepted the obvious: that my happiness had always been an illusion. It was just a story I told myself to survive, a fantasy invented by an isolated and imaginative boy. Clix had constructed a dream world because he had no other choice.

Later, the major work of my adult life would become being 'normal' again – or at least someone who nearly passed for it. Years spent becoming just another eccentric, vaguely posh Englishman with floppy hair and wonky teeth. I taught myself to hug people, to look them in the eye, to shake hands firmly: to fake confidence until it finally became real. Eventually I stood tall again; I regrew my strength and at least some of my looks – gangly and odd though I would remain. Always a freak in some people's eyes (to this day, strangers sometimes insult me in the street).

– I had been left to fix myself once more; to assemble a version that could learn to survive, from whatever relics came to hand. (Aren't we all the same, in the junk shops of our solitary hearts?) But long before then, a darkness was hurtling towards me: a shadow. And its name was… *Dad*.

****

Throughout my youth, I felt his absence on more occasions than I care to remember, of course. He would pass without speaking or even looking at me, *en route* to the star maps in his study. Mum was right: I was invisible, insignificant. Perhaps she had cursed this into being for trapping her in a loveless home.

– *My father the wizard, my mother the witch.*

Once in my teens, Dad asked me to tell him about something I was working on: a picture, a story, a classical guitar piece. I was taken aback, happy for a moment that something I was doing had even registered with him. But as I opened my mouth to speak, he left the house and slammed the front door in my face. I watched through the prismatic glass as a dozen images of my father's back walked slowly away towards town, like he was ambling towards Hiroshima.

– *The white flash in the sky; the grey dust that had once been lives.*

But why was this happening? Wasn't this simply life with a traumatised man – a savant, a dysfunctional logician? Or the detritus of a grim adolescence? Partly. But the fact is, I knew exactly what his silence meant. At least, the one that lurked beyond the horrors of atomic war.

– *Dad wanted my silence too.*

Other events triggered the same night-woven flashbacks. One day in my late teens, my father – the man who never spoke – spent a whole hour on the phone with the teenaged son of a new, middle-aged friend of his. Some man from the country with a double-barrelled name, who passed the receiver to the boy.

This was one of the mysterious acquaintances that flared briefly for Dad over the years, like matches in a rainstorm. Always they were swiftly forgotten – after some sleight or mistake on their part, no doubt.

Dad listened attentively to another man's son – if that is who he was – and smiled warmly, indulgently, as I had never seen him do before; that old photographic charm flashing in the shadows. His voice became silky, bewitched… almost flirtatious. But who *were* these people? This man, this boy who was taking music lessons while I was an accomplished player? Who were they to my father?

At one point, Dad planned to go on holiday with them on his own, but Mum intervened, and they were never heard from or spoken of again. Then she whisked me away on a half-remembered vacation herself: just the two of us, walking by the sea – me hunched and dead-eyed in an anorak. The sense that I was being shielded from secrets was impossible to ignore.

In Dad's study one day I saw a notebook lying open, with the words, 'In for a penny, in for a pound, it's LOVE that makes the world go round' circled in black ink. But which of them did he love in place of his entire extended family: the man? *Or the boy?*

Yet explanations are not as simple as they first appear. Because there was someone else too: a woman. Mum thought she worked at Heals in the Tottenham Court Road. Dad had smiled and nodded at her furtively once, something even I noticed. Was there another family, another life? *Did my father have another son, one he doted on and indulged?*

Then I remembered the times my aunt would back away from Dad sometimes, in the kitchen at her country house (he would profess his love for her later[13]). Mum twitched the curtains daily in search of the truth. She spied on people, stood on chairs with binoculars, yet it always eluded her, as Mrs Ward loomed over the fence from her garden two feet higher than ours, beaming like Joyce Grenfell.

My father's oddness and secrecy deepened Mum's suspicions. Once he didn't tell us that he had to go into hospital for a major operation; later he pretended to drive to work for months after he had been made redundant. We had no idea.

So, who *was* this man who called himself my father? Every signpost about him pointed down different paths, some into deepest shadow. He was the Quantum Uncertainty Principle made flesh: the more we knew one thing about him – or thought we did – the less everything else made sense.

During the long, troubled years of my adolescence, I began to feel more like a ghost than a teenager, as if my parents and I were spirits trapped in an old, dark house, far from the corporeal world. Family meals were like seances at which we tried to contact the living.

"It doesn't say much about that boy that he would be jealous of *someone like you*," Dad hissed at me once when a classmate complimented my writing. One winter's evening, he pulled out the main electrical fuse and plunged the entire house into darkness rather than tell a friend of mine to go home. It was terrifying.

So, it is night now. And I come to the demon crouched on my chest: to the incubus, perhaps. It is an earlier, much darker memory. One that clutches at me, tearing at my clothes, leaving them threadbare and tattered. It is fragmented, the complete picture forever just out of reach. But it is there. It has *always* been there.

This is what crept into my life as a teenager and turned me sad, inward, and desolate. This is what made a happy, clever, creative boy that any parent should have loved and been proud of into a ghost – a revenant and spectre, like the monk I once saw on the oak-panelled stairs at Reigate Priory, all evanescent, shimmering, dancing, and grey.

Come with me.

I am walking in the Castle Grounds with my father, at the age of eight. It is the early Seventies, and a huge owl is hunched high in a tree, its back turned.

Another middle-aged man is waiting at the folly's gateway. My father seems to know him; an arranged meeting, it seems – odd, as my misanthropic parents had no friends at all locally, and socialised with no one. Normally it is just me and Dad in this godforsaken place. In the trees and hidden paths. Ever lost in the shadows.

Two much older boys are with the man: teenagers, seventeen or eighteen, perhaps his sons. They pace around me, circling like wolves. Now I am climbing the hill to the castle keep with these strangers, led away by the hand while my father stands below, waiting, in his architect's shirtsleeves and cravat.

– *I am a gift*. This time.

Now I am standing in a thicket with my trousers down, surrounded by thorns. Someone is right behind me, the others nearby. I am frightened and crying, in pain. *The bloody rose.*

I have no other memory of that day, except going back down the hill with those men, with the wolves of Reigate town. It is a blank, like over-exposed film.

Then they handed me back to my father.

– *And the Spirit of Summer hides his head in his hands. And weeps for all that is lost now, forever.*

What I'm certain of is this: if I was out with my father in the weeks that followed and we saw that mysterious trio, I would point at them and shout words I have no memory of using or even *hearing* before at that age: "You! You dirty pricks! Batty pricks!" until we never walked out together again. "You *mustn't cause a scene in public*," Dad hissed. Clever boy.

I used to call them "my bad friends" – words that made my mother freeze one day and stare, frightened, at my father. I had no other language to describe them, no concept of malign intent in my happy-go-lucky Clix world. But for years afterwards, I was haunted by terrifying images that I struggled to place or comprehend.

And by the growing sense – the *understanding* – that my father had taken me to a garden to be raped by three men.

****

His door slammed shut on me from then on, while I went back to my boyhood world of spaceships, paintings, and music. For a while, at least, I forgot. Or rather, I ushered those moments away, into songs, stories, and poetry: secret messages to myself and my friends.

The first song I ever wrote as a boy was called 'Screaming Inside': *"I was always a child, such a child in my understanding... but now I'm screaming, screaming inside."* Yet no one heard what I was trying to tell them, though I was hiding in plain sight. Because if you are a storyteller, soon everything becomes a fiction.

But in my disintegrating teens, this resurfacing memory – this *realisation* – began to radiate from within. Like atomic waste, something you can bury in the deepest, safest places, but never destroy. My father would have known that better than most.

And that vulnerability, that damage, itself attracted bullies in the years that followed: insecure men, narcissists, sociopaths, and egotists; people who needed a punchbag and someone to laugh at so they could feel good about themselves. I sometimes welcomed them as friends, mistaking their rampant insecurities for confidence and strength.

The world is full of such arrogant straw men: in government, in business, in the arts. And all bullies are riven with insecurity, by the need to hurt for self-gratification; becoming the teeth to match their own wounds. (You've met them too, I know.)

Back in my boyhood, the older man would be waiting in a car outside my middle-school gates sometimes, offering me sweets to get in with him; I kept walking. I'm not certain I would be here today had I not done so, because one morning when Mum was walking me to school, the same car mounted the pavement and drove straight at me, accelerating. She pulled me out of the way just in time.

– Just a small-town accident, no doubt. Just another shadow in the creaking, threadbare hallway. It was never mentioned again.

Now Clix was a marked boy: a target, with crosshairs on his ass – and his life. *("And the night reached out, and then I reached out… and we touched"* – another early song.)

Predators like this were everywhere in 1970s Surrey towns, behind the creosoted fences, the Conservative Clubs, and the manicured hedges. The stooped vulture in the schools' outfitters who would pat my bottom slowly, saying, "Look at his little seat". The physics teacher who stood behind me in the snow, breathing heavily, as he made me bend over in

89

my singlet and shorts to shovel coal – my punishment for dancing with happiness one day. The art teacher who grabbed Danny's crotch as he was walking through a door, telling him he was "bad meat".

Did experiences like this make me – or any of us – gay? No, *why would they*? If anything, they would surely have pushed me the other way. Being gay has nothing to do with stalking kids for kicks.

I've always known that I'm gay, certainly long before any of this happened; it was a flame I centred in my chest and carried proudly in the headwind. I was born that way, *a little madam*, and my father knew it. Even at middle-school.

– Spinning and jumping in front of the class, and rigging toy theatres with Christmas lights. Gazing at astronauts in Will Robinson's spacesuit, and singing to Belle, like Sebastian in the mountains. Playing 'Phones' to Troy Tempest as Marina swam, mute and glamorous in Stingray's ocean. On the Cannonball Express with Casey Jones, wisecracking with Spider-Man and Commander Straker. Yet coveting my sister's kohl-eyed ballerinas: the Black Swan and the Sugar-plum Fairy.

Clix, the idea of a child, sleepless and frightened in his father's arms, carried back to bed in search of dreams. On white horses of the mind, but now lying in the thorns, aged eight, and bleeding. Forever broken, like his parents' war-blighted lives.

****

There were others like me at senior school, of course. We would nod and smile at each other discreetly, but always ignore the subtext – a held glance in the art room, in the garden behind the swimming pool; conversations with covert meanings. Some were good friends, and others fellow travellers on a hidden but, for most of us, completely unexplored road. It was the 1970s and Eighties and we were all terrified – of AIDS, of ridicule, shame, and discovery.

Except John Poncier, who once paraded the entire length of the school in a satin dress and full makeup, carrying a handbag. He wore a green carnation to honour Oscar Wilde, walking slowly with his head held high as a thousand boys laughed, jeered, banged on the windows, and spat at him. Then he marched out of the grounds and disappeared forever, never once looking back. The most heroic act I have ever seen.

Once I accepted it in my late twenties and early thirties, being gay has been nothing but a source of happiness, friendship, love, and peace to me – the odd broken heart and messy break-up aside. I am a better, stronger, kinder, and more tolerant person because of it, and no longer display that most damaging prejudice: hatred of the self.

– Walking home from Danny's house, up Cronks Hill in the dark, hiding my face from the moonlit windows, from the

headlights of passing cars. But the moon was empty now:
mournful, silvered, and alone. Yet still somehow as bright.

Understand this: you can't make someone gay by abusing them; or by grooming them, assaulting them, raping them, or depriving them of paternal support. All you do is fill a gay person with self-loathing when they could be full of confidence and pride. Some of us are abused *because* we are gay, not to make us so. And some of us are just abused.

I've met dozens of men over the years who have had similar experiences to mine: abuse, distant fathers, rape, emotional mothers (why wouldn't they be emotional?), and *all* of them are straight. Scratch the surface of many a quiet or angry man and you'll find an abuse victim.

Gay men aren't made by predators, distant fathers, or (as misogynists claim) by overbearing mothers; but many are certainly hurt by them. And straight men are too. And lest we forget, every woman and girl in the world has been hit on by older men at some point in their lives – every one of them. Something the homophobes conveniently ignore, as they wolf-whistle at teenage girls.

The problem isn't predatory gay men. *It's predatory men.*

Back in the Seventies and Eighties, the straight men in my world were mostly violent, while others were just old, war-damaged, angry, and bitter. The physics teacher who punched my lippy friend Small Paul in the face, knocking his NHS glasses across the room; the history master who slammed my friend Alan against a wall and held him by his throat until he began to turn blue (Alan later joined the Army to give his own violence meaning); the young chemistry teacher who smacked me viciously about the head with his fists for daring to speak on his hallowed rugby field, frozen as it was in the January gloom. Another barely concealed psychopath.

The incoherent rage of pathetic, insecure, fragile men, who should all have been in prison. In a sense, I suppose some were.

I was too, until I set myself free and gave myself permission to be happy.

To *live* again.

Bookends

CHALK DUST

One January morning I was walking alone across the empty playground at senior school – late for another lesson, of course – when I heard a voice calling from somewhere. "Coo-ee!" it said. I looked around. "Coo-ee!" it came again. *"Over here!"*

A languid arm dangled from a high window in the fog, and beckoned me to come forward. Now I could see a whole classroom full of pupils, looking as puzzled as I was at the gangly limb and long, commanding finger.

I walked a few steps more and looked up. It was Aubrey Scrase – 'Aubs' for short, our long-limbed, goofy Classics teacher. He would hurl chalk rubbers at boys' heads, when he wasn't teaching us about gonorrhoea and syphilis in Religious Studies.

"Oh... *hello*," I said, nervously. He was hanging half out of a window, after all.

"Hold out your hand," said Aubs, as his Latin class looked at each other, mouths agape. I did. He dropped an old shiny sixpence into it, which I still have to this day. Then he stuck out his tongue at me and blew a raspberry.

"Happy birthday," said Aubs.

Intermission

MISS SKILTON

At the age of eighteen, I won a national short story prize. My piece was a tribute to an elderly woman, Edith Skilton, who I used to visit in my mid-teens. She would come alive in her sickbed as I spoke to her, and I would glimmer again too as she spun stories of her youth. Somehow an old lady who was letting go of life, and a boy whose light was dimming, found each other exactly when they needed to.

I loved her very much. Here is the story I wrote for her.

****

PRIMA SINGS, THE AUTUMN FALLS
by Christopher J Middleton, aged 18

Miss Edie spoke of miracles.

Summer had come late, and the ground felt airy and clinging, neither soil nor leaf-mould, as if compounded of dust and bone meal and the dried husks of thunderclouds.

Click ran homewards down the bluff, his soft bones proud in the flesh he would carry into the earth and give back to the land by sleeping.

The house was a grounded ship, its timbers powdered and ashen. When the sun was at full mast, you could hear them above the porch swing, creaking, while his father tested the winds with his forgotten hands, naming the seasons Good Weather or Bad.

Click shook his thatch of hair and ran into the house. He was slower than the others, for he had lived in this house – and the house in him – with its astrolabes, sextants, and bottles to trap wandering spirits.

Click spat then ran out back, accepting the summons like birdsong.

– *Miss Edie? You there?*

She lay on a daybed, all sepia and windfallen. Click was sorry; sorry she had lost her bloom and fallen. Some days she wore daisies. Then, as morning swooned towards noontime, she added bluebells and violets and little seedling bells, and Click would dance around her as if she was Winter disguised as Spring. From her bed, she put up her hands to feel him there, supposing he was her spirit come wandering back from the hills.

– *Click, my Click? You chosen summer yet, my boy?*
Sucking her teeth with his name on her lips and her hair brushed pearly and beautiful.

– *I'm here, Miss Edie. And I brought your Bible too.*

It was a seamless, cloud-borne day; a glassy round where warm winds blew. Miss Edie was old and speaking freely

all at once and Click was
a ghost at her bedside: an essence and the sum of his parts,
standing beside her in the clear-moving green afternoon.

Entering, he thought: Who will be here in years to come to
grieve for her that went before? And will storms form in
these rafters, scaring birds away into all eternity, to rain on
the father with the winter-cracked face and the dim white
wings that failed behind his eyes?

– *Read*, motioned Miss Edie, knowing all this but still
smiling. *Tell me The Good Book.*

– *"Mother was like a grapevine, planted near a stream.
Because there was plenty of water, the vine was clothed in
leaves and fruits, and its branches were strong and grew to
be royal sceptres…"*

– *Ezekiel! Nineteen.*

– *That was beautiful, Miss Edie*, Click whispered.

– *Memory often is, child*, she preened. *Come: let us walk
outside.*

Summer winds held a pale moon aloft like air in the hollow
of a wave. Father sat on the porch, lost on some long
voyage of thought. *It was here they had said goodbye*, he
remembered, *waving after him for as long as they could
see his back*. He had sailed on alone into the cold country,
then, where men are grounded and grow old.

– *Speak*, he thought. *Speak if you can hear me, all my old
friends…*

Click heard his father cry out, once, and turn three times in his sleep.

Miss Edie knew the heart of the forest; knew it might send a snake pricking at your heels; knew when to be quiet, as if she were in love; knew to name the flowers under her breath as she curtsied through the tangles, spangling her rusty parasol.

– *Saturnus, Illyricum, Cloth of Gold... That's a pretty one! Lutea, Zonatus, Maiden's Blush!*

She didn't know what lay ahead, only that she must tend and collect and prod and fuss and, if she turned back at last with a sense of her place in things, that she would reveal not herself but the glory of the forest.

Now Click had come to the Place of Two Worlds. Down at the softwood jetty, the centre of the forest widened like an iris above the water. Miss Edie picked her way among pendulous grasses and nodding wildflowers. From here, thought Click, a bird might fly to all things – to river, sky, and treasures of the sea – fly with drops of light to bathe herself and administer to her plumage.

– *Now,* he thought. *Here.* And, sucking a deep breath into his lungs, he threw back his head and cried out the one name that seemed perfect to him. But silently, so as not to disturb his father whose eyes were heavy and adorned with sleep. He called it secretly; inwardly.

– *Prima.*

Click could not summon her at first; it was as though the forest held too many ghosts for her. But as he held his breath the lone swift came in a shrieking black arc to scythe the treetops with a dry fluttering of wings and call Click deeper into the forest.

He had found the bird dazed and flightless on the ground one day, her struggling wings too long for her to take off. So, Click had picked Prima up and thrown her back into the sky. Now he imagined that the swift he had called out to ever since was that same bird, as she wheeled and screamed above the high poplars.

– *That boy needs discipline*, his father mumbled, the dead land beneath his eyes. On the porch at his feet, a grey cat mewled about and stood up graceful.

Let him be, said Miss Edie at the old man's shoulder.
Discipline?
Discipline is fifty acres of barren land.

The river ran wrinkled and sweet to breathe with a half-drowsy smile. Click ducked and jumped and hunted footprints smaller than a bird's while the turning sky descended, hung with clouds and darkening.

He said the words over and over to himself, until he had them refined: "*Mother was like a grapevine planted near a stream. Because there was plenty of water, the vine was clothed in leaves and fruits and its branches were strong and grew to be royal sceptres...*"

And the dream soared above the forest, for a moment that drew his arm upwards like a child's in sleep. Then Click threw himself on the dead land and wept for the father who rarely spoke. And for the mother who had never said goodbye.

Act Five

Radio Clix

If time ran backwards, every day would end at sunrise.

I had Owen; and I had many schoolfriends – even in my darkest days. But once home, I spent much of my time alone, improvising the future I live in today. Yet one thing was clear to me from an early age: I needed to contact the outside world somehow, and escape the old, dark house in which I found myself. But this was in the days long before the internet, laptops, social networks, and smartphones.

So, at the age of eight, I built a crystal set. I bolted capacitors, diodes, and transistors onto a piece of chipboard, then grabbed the 1940s earpiece I had found in a junk shop and listened. The first words I heard were, "This is the World Service"; I must have tuned in exactly on the hour. I had somehow reached far beyond the tree of ghosts at my window and contacted the planet. Or rather, it had spoken to me with a rather British-sounding voice.

Then one day, my crystal set picked up a numbers station: a German voice intoning, "*Sieben, acht, neun, zehn... ende*", as though my parents' war had reached through decades of static to a boy's bedroom in the 1970s.

Timothy – Mrs Ward's son who lived next door in a room full of oscilloscopes and vacuum tubes – told me I had wired it up all wrong and that's why it was speaking

German. Before I could point out the flaw in his theory, he took my circuit apart and rebuilt it. Of course, it never worked again.

Undeterred, I built a whole radio station in my bedroom from an old Roberts radio, an electronics kit, and the skeleton of an umbrella which I covered in tinfoil. This was the aerial; I had seen photos of the Jodrell Bank space telescope.

– I was just a boy – Clicky, or Clix for short, always full of hope and laughter. Just eight years old and trying to contact the outside world through my window, through the grasping, haunted elm.

I lived in a town so quiet, so deserted, that playgrounds were empty, and I would sit alone on the swings while my mother watched. Now I was calling for help, for human contact.

With my transmitter rigged in the window at night – umbrella pointing at the stars – I could broadcast anywhere on the medium wave over a range of about half a mile. I would tune into the radios of passing cars, and say, *"Hello, my name is Christopher... can anybody help me?"* Then I would read the drivers stories as they sat at the traffic lights – allegories of lost boys, perhaps. Christ knows what they must have thought.

Then one day, the police came; but not to arrest my father. They were making enquiries in the area about a boy's spectral voice appearing on top of radio stations whenever cars pulled up at the crossing. Mum told them to go away and stop being ridiculous: her son was just an eight-year-old child. Did they think he was a boffin, or some kind of genius?

But she knew it was me. The little boy who wrote comedy sketches, short stories, and plays, dressing up as all the different characters, wearing disguises inspired by Lon Chaney; the boy who performed *The Twelve Days of Christmas* with a choir of giggling friends, changing the words to a list of ever more tongue-twisting, absurd consumer items while the headmaster scowled and the audience fell about; the boy who built transmitters and invented machines out of discarded junk and somehow made them work; the boy who played classical guitar at Morning Assembly, aged nine, until the chattering stopped and the room fell silent. I've always been able to do that with a guitar.

My song went:

"Tune in, to short-wave radio
Listen to the air, and the world
fills you with other voices
and you're diving in deep for pearls.

I first heard your voice as I listened one night
and if I reached for the light, you'd say
'No, no, no, don't turn me over'.

Listen and the ocean will lead you through the night,
with all of her voices whispering, 'I love you'."

I play it still.

The little boy who taught slower classmates to read and write at primary school; who stood up to bullies in the playground and dealt with others' problems when they came to him for advice. The boy who middle-school teachers described as a budding writer, actor, film director, or scientist – later as a dark horse and a prodigy. The boy who sat quietly in his room experimenting with tape loops and headphones at the age of eight, while his parents screamed at each other in the hall below. The boy who played coffee-tin drums in the garden while Lois sang and smiled and grew an inch in confidence. The boy whose father used to snap his fingers to summon him, like he was calling a dog in Priory Park.

The child who had all his hope, magick, and laughter snuffed out by two miserable, war-damaged people and a town full of violent men. *The useless, stupid, insignificant boy.*

Later, books, music, and movies offered me an escape into a world of drama, glamour, and the safety of my dreams: Clix, the boy with a universe in his head that was full of fire, poetry, melody, and wonder. *"You've got to get in to get out,"* as Peter Gabriel sang. So, I got in, deeper and deeper, until I finally escaped.

I remember seeing Sparks on our black-and-white telly and feeling my world explode into colour. Roxy Music followed: at just eight years old I would stomp into Rhythms on Church Street and demand to hear *Street Life* and *Pyjamarama* in the listening booth, while the glamour-girl cover of *Stranded* made my mother scream.

There were Bowie and Major Tom, lost astronauts in tin cans, and Kate Bush spinning a world of stories from the suburban air, calling me away to the dreamtime. I ran with them as fast as I could, to libraries and bookshops, to cinemas, guitars, synthesisers, and cassette recorders. So many doors to a world that could never be destroyed. If I could hide myself there, I would always be safe.

In 2014 at Hammersmith Apollo, I finally saw Kate live at her comeback show, *Before the Dawn*. The beautiful woman with the dressing-up box, the siren whose voice had lifted me up so many times as she span through the forest of her imagination, was now a middle-aged mum with a loving son at her side. How wonderful.

As I watched, alone above the stage, Kate sat at her piano and sang these words to me, though hundreds of other broken people believed she was singing just for them, as she always has.

> *"Only you can do something about it*
> *There's no one there, my friend, any better…"*
> (Among Angels – Kate Bush)

"I've travelled so far to get here," said the American stranger sat next to me. "Never thought I'd see the day."

"I know just what you mean," I said.

Setting the broken free. I had been through another rough time: the death of my mother; the brief, disastrous rapprochement with my father, which had reopened a hundred wounds; the loss of Danny, one of my closest friends; plus, a client had stolen a valuable idea from me, leaving me with nothing, then fired me out of spite. All this had happened in a matter of weeks. But though tears were streaming down my face as Kate sang, I felt myself coming alive again, filling with an ancient warmth and hope.

The kind I had as a little boy.

– He's here again, the man with the child in his eyes.

You see, I have always been optimistic. I am always looking for ways to make something, to build something new. Searching for light in the darkness, no matter what, stands at the core of who I am; or of what little is left. Clix taught me that, and I keep his restless, creative spirit alive at the centre of the man I am today. He deserved better than what his parents did to him – the rape, the abuse, the emotional violence. So, I try to make him proud.

I live in his world to this day, the one I built for myself. It is home, as it always has been. Sometimes friends come and go, carrying drums and guitars. A few will stay for a while, and it means everything to me to pick out a tune with them. But I am still there when they leave – typing, drawing, and composing. I am here now, gazing out beyond the pier to where France lies propped on an elbow. Rain-swept England, forever watching the sea.

Sometimes I look around at my world of stories, pictures, guitars, and ideas: at the things I chose for myself in life, at the rocket I built and used to fly away from pain. Or I look over my shoulder at my little rock band, scan my magazine articles and books, see my audience at conferences and shows, and the stages full of professors, astronauts, technologists, and musicians I talk to and write about. And I know that, somewhere lost in time, Clix is smiling.

– *He's here again,* one last time.

He giggles at the wild ride I've had – at my ridiculous adventures, the scrapes I've got into, the cities I've seen, the people I've met. Then he nods, puts his hand on my arm, and says, "It's alright, you know." And I know this because I *am* him, and he is me. Then he puts his headphones back on as the old tape recorder unspools, reads his book, and disappears forever.

"I did my best, kid," I say.

Clix knows that I've walked the length of Manhattan, and through Central Park in the snow. That I've watched spaceships being built. That I've left my footprints on Mars – in Pasadena, where NASA tests the atomic rovers. That I've stood at the Center of the Universe[14].

He knows I've learned the streets of Paris, Barcelona, San Francisco, and New York like the back of my hand. That I've met astrophysicists, tech geniuses, astronauts, and men who've turned themselves into androids. I've helped abuse victims and listened to their music when they were unable to speak from inner pain. I've heard Buzz Aldrin talk about the moon, then shaken his hand and thanked him, *my Captain*. I've gazed across the water in Shanghai, climbed the Hollywood Hills, and stood atop Table Mountain. I've been to outrageous clubs with men dressed as angels. I've walked my sister up the aisle in place of my father, welcomed my African brother, and watched my niece grow into a beautiful woman. I've gazed at the Milky Way on a volcanic island as my husband made love to me. I've seen a thousand wild cats in a flash of lightning. I've swum in transparent seas, crossed oceans, sped in Venetian water taxis, and made people cry, smile, and laugh.

I've skated into a hundred sunrises. I've heard my song on the radio being played by Tom Robinson. I've made rowdy pubs shout for an encore. I've sat in Abbey Road listening to old Beatles recordings, drunk coffee with David Gilmour, and put my feet up in Peter Gabriel's recording studio. I've edited books and magazines, and published a few of my own. I've succeeded and I've failed, and I've learned from my countless, stupid mistakes. I've stood people back on their feet and helped them see the positive. I've drunk and I've smoked, and I've watched atoms being smashed together in subterranean chambers. I've shot Lauren Bacall with a film camera. I've loved beautiful men, and one or two have even loved me back. I've married a man who adores me. I've honoured my parents in public, scattered their ashes in the English green, then walked away, clapping the dust from my hands.

I have danced, and laughed, and sobbed, and fallen, and mourned, and shouted, and moshed, and savoured, and argued, and marvelled, and punched the air at a thousand gigs. I've even owned a real robot, just like Will Robinson. And above all, I am happy.

I have *lived*, and I am alive.

I am *kintsugi*. Broken, but held together with gold.

Bookends:

TO THE MOON, BACKWARDS

I don't remember becoming middle-aged, the precise
moment it happened. We all consent to it, I suppose, on the
day we decide to keep going, to throw in our lot with the
world.

Perhaps it happens when you wander off the high street
into one of those covered malls that no one shops in. You
know the places from walking past them a thousand times:
the empty chessboard floor – no queens or knights; the
shop full of toiletries in thick orange boxes; the barber's
chair no one sits in; the gallery full of premiership décor;
the outfitters selling floral shirts, and Italian jackets you've
not quite heard of. A mall that says a gangster is in town,
one you will meet some day in the dark. Mr Big with a
flick-knife and a reckoning. He finds us all eventually.

These malls are time-traps for the unwary. They are gravity
wells, portals that transport us towards old age. Once
you've entered one you are displaced forever, always
slightly out of sync with the world. You can go home
again, you can return to the high street and those old,
familiar places, but you have been changed indelibly. Now
people bump into you in shopping centres but still don't see
you. There's the same face in the shaving mirror, but you
no longer recognise yourself in photographs. You measure
your life in coffee spoons, but the jar is emptying. You

have become unknown to yourself; you are invisible to everyone but baristas.

Andreas is my local barista. He is Albanian, dark, and pretty, with stubble designed to accentuate his cheekbones. He slinks like a cat with its tail up, dancing on the lightest feet. His eyes glitter in his private night, because he hates people but is paid to be charming. Real cats can hear the ticking of time, but Andreas cannot: he does not see that his own hair is thinning, that he is five years from being empty and disappointed; sitting on his own at Legends, getting drunk enough to screw the local psycho. His boss at the café is wiry and hideous but walks with the alpha confidence of a prize fighter, hiding something big in his jeans. For him, everything is a transaction.

But behind these tired eyes and wrinkled visage, I am still the 30-something who could walk into the Two Brewers on Clapham High Street in the Nineties and early Noughties, and leave with the most beautiful man there. Like Simon, the blonde suedehead who stood next to me one night with his eyes sparkling – next day I walked to his door with a glass of champagne. Or Duncan who smiled as he danced alone, writing poetry in his head.

At work I met Kev, my ageless American friend, who for thirty years has looked like a 1950s CIA agent. I still have the photo I took of him with his hands in Jimmy Stewart's palm prints outside the Chinese Theatre in LA. Later we avoided the rocks on Mulholland Drive and gazed at the Hollywood sign as it shivered in the heat. He threw a book at my head once, but took time to select the right title – a good definition of love.

And then there was Ronald, the urbane Guyanan who was five times happy at my side. Paren, who invited me back to my place – I told him I was going there anyway, but he was welcome to tag along. He left chips on my doorstep and stayed for five years, gifting me an Indian family and friends. And Ian, my unrequited love – the cause of me shouting at myself one day in the mirror; he fell for a man who was his double, which helped. He saw his own reflection, smiled, and jumped into bed with it.

Vittorio on the slow boat to France and the fast train to Paris. He laughed at the drag queen in Pigalle to show he wasn't gay, then we slept in each other's arms – he was a Catholic, of course. He waited for me for two hours at Montparnasse station. For that I sent him a Christmas card in Rome.

W, the Singaporean designer, forever poised between handsome and pretty. He'd book the best hotels and lie in my arms as we gazed from their windows. Today he's the multimillionaire head of a corporation, a distant voice on WhatsApp from stunning apartments. But now he hides his ageing face, so I talk to his memory as we catch up on news.

Martin, who was so beautiful I became witty enough to laugh him home. With Jamie, his equal, I sat in a moonbeam on Brighton beach as the tide came in. Next morning, we found ourselves in a room full of bees that fuzzed and crackled in the summer heat.

Or there was Andrew, the model I picked up while drunk at Popstarz, then woke to find I was in bed with an angel. Eddy and Eddy, the double act, and Brion with the Islington apartment full of Old Masters he faked. He snapped at me once, so I didn't tell him we had passed Madonna on Place Vendôme and she had smiled at us.

James, the laughing South Londoner and Britpop fan, who came out as bald one night and left his hairpiece on a lampstand. Joe, who danced and smiled, then danced some more: I loved you. Pablo whose golden eyes flashed green with jealousy, and Hiren whose eyes are sapphire – my beautiful old friend; I love to make you laugh. And Noom, the moon backwards, with the wicked grin. When he laughed, he jumped up and down, then climbed back into bed and kissed me.

And then there is Stu. At 2am on Brighton beach, as the tide turned, I told him about Captain Buzz. It was the night we got engaged.

So many stories… all of them happy, in the end.

"A skinny mocha, please. To take out."
"Do you want that to go?"
"…yes please."
"Can you *imagine*?" Andreas whispers to Igor, pulling a face and gesturing at me. *"Can you imagine?"*

Afterword

Hello. My name is Christopher.

This is my truth. This is my voice speaking again at last, my tinfoil aerial open against the glass. Broadcasting from Radio Clix.

Can you hear me, driver at the traffic lights, revving your engine and waiting? Can you see the little boy in the window, spinning stories to the songless hills? Can you see the stars wheel about his head? Can you see the moon place coins in his eyes? Can you see his body, lying in the rose garden? And can you see the fire in him gutter and bend?

I know you can. Because I know you are watching.

But who are you? And what do you want from him?

After all, he is just an insignificant boy.

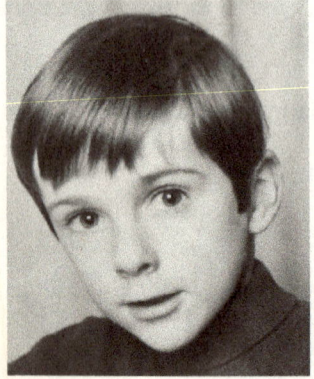

Acknowledgements

With thanks to my sister, for her memories, love, and support – though what she learned shocked her. And to David Jones, the young teacher (now retired) who stood by me at senior school. The line 'they should all have been in prison' is his.

This book is dedicated to my dear friend Mike Jenkins, a beautiful soul and wonderful poet, who has helped me through many a difficult time. And to Mikey East, who fights for life harder than any man I've known, yet is always smiling. I love you both very much.

And to all my friends, today and over the years. Some are gone – Danny, Martin, Paul, Anthony, Mark, and Jamie – and some are missing. Each one of you has meant more to me than I can say.

And finally, to Tracey Thorn, whose memoir 'Another Planet', convinced me I could write a small, local story that still deserved to be told. Thank you.

Now, this is Radio Clix, signing off.

C, L, I...! C, K, Y!

NOTES

1: Clicky was also the name of a clockwork boy clown in a series of children's books by Enid Blyton. The illustrations by Molly Brett resembled me as a little boy.

2: A Stellaphone (the Dictaphone mentioned later was a 1958 Time-Master). While writing this memoir, I googled 1950s tape recorders. The first image that came up was not only of the same model, but also of the exact one I had as a little boy, damaged in all the same places. It was for sale on eBay; I bought it, of course. Incredibly, the tape, apparently not played since I gave the machine to a jumble sale in the early Eighties, contains a recording of Radio Clix. "Hello... my name is Christopher..." An extraordinary set of coincidences.

3: This is true, as well as an apt metaphor. Aged eight, I planted seeds from a fir cone I had picked up in the Castle Grounds with my father. (It may have been on the same walk that would change the course of my life.) By the 2010s, last time I saw it, the tree towered over my parents' old house.

4: We don't know if Dad did work at Bletchley Park, only that my sister saw him in a photograph onscreen in a documentary about Turing and his team. We have no idea of my father's whereabouts from 1940-41 (aged 15-16) at St Paul's Cathedral, to his service in Japan in 1946. And I no longer care (please don't write to me about it!).

5: My father's funeral took place on the Summer Solstice, 2021. His ashes were scattered in the trees, on a hill he would stare at from his window. I believe he knew he would end up there.

6: After Mum died, my father asked me to help him design and publish his book on HG Wells, duping me into believing he was trying to make amends after years of estrangement. He then told me he had found someone else to do it: a final act of needless cruelty. The bond with his son, and with the rest of his family, had no meaning for him at all.

7: At the time of writing, La Trobe's hidden toyshop in Reigate (which closed in 1982 after fifty-six years, when its elderly owners retired) is now a local branch of The Samaritans. Please seek help if you need it. Never give up on yourself, no matter what.

8: Will Robinson, played by Billy Mumy in the original TV series 'Lost in Space', was another childhood hero of mine: a boy who, like me, used his brains to survive. My love of robots stems from the show.

9: 'Captain Buzz Forever': I later wrote a song with that title, celebrating Aldrin's slow walk back to sobriety. My hero was a poet at heart, as well as a scientist, pilot, and adventurer. The words "magnificent desolation", his description of the moon on 20 July 1969, are surely some of the most perfect ever spoken off the cuff.

10: Mum also exiled her brother from the family, my Uncle Jim, because he had married a woman she disapproved of. Meanwhile, my father ignored his two sisters and their large, extended families for decades, because they disagreed with him once. I grew up not knowing most of my aunts, uncles, and cousins.

11: My mother's memory of the Great Train Robber had tragic echoes a decade later. Unknown to us, Biggs' girlfriend was the daughter of my primary school headmaster. One day in the 1970s, Mr Powell was found dead in the lake opposite the school. His death was never explained.

12: While swimming in the sea on a school trip to France, aged ten, I foolishly tried to splash a friend, David, by throwing a rock into the water near him. But he turned and ran towards me in the split second after I had thrown it, so it struck him on the leg. The idea that I had hurt another person, albeit without meaning to, horrified me. So, the memory of him smiling and waving at me as he won a race later is one that I treasure. (But I see it now: our middle-aged teachers weren't showing us ancient history on our trip to the wartime Normandy beaches. They were showing us their recent memories.)

13: My aunt certainly didn't return any feelings Dad might have had for her: she adored her husband, my late uncle (and my father's only long-term friend), who passed away when I was 12. Indeed, she spent the last twenty years of her life mourning his loss. Once when I asked her about Dad's strange behaviour, she thought hard for a second and said, "Well, he's certainly a repressed... something."

14. The official Center of the Universe is marked by a plaque on the floor in Mission Control at NASA's Jet Propulsion Laboratory in Pasadena, in the mountains above LA.

I was at the JPL on the day they tested the Mars helicopter. And I left my footprint in the red dust on the Mars backlot where they test-drive the atomic-powered rovers: I was perhaps the first man in a tailored suit on Mars. A few days later, I was at NASA in Houston on the day the US announced it was returning to the moon.

Clix would have been so happy – and so proud. I felt connected to him that day: I had come full circle. The man he invented all those years ago had finally given him the future he dreamed of when he found himself lost in space, spinning in the darkness.

So, never forget who you are, dear reader. Not even for a moment. Dream yourself a future, and escape towards it, running. Even if the present seems horrible and bleak.

I wish you well. And thank you for reading my story.

It has taken me a lifetime. But finally, I am free.

Chris Middleton, October 2023.